Lindsay Cameron

The 5 Stages of Missions

First print 2007.

Copyright © 2007, 2012, 2018, 2021 Lindsay Cameron.
All rights reserved.

Scripture quotations are taken from the HOLY BIBLE, NEW INTERNATIONAL VERSION. Copyright © 1973, 1978, 1984 International Bible Society. Used by permission of Zondervan Bible Publishers.

International Standard Book Number
ISBN-13: 97800980417265

Cypress
Project

Published by
Cypress Project
Australia

https://cypressproject.com.au

Acknowledgements

The 5 Stages of Missions has achieved the current evolution because of the thoughtful and honest interaction of my work colleagues, both in North America and in the African churches. Furthermore, this publication has become a reality because of the discipline of my studies at the University of South Africa, under the guidance of my supervisor, Professor Willem Saayman. I am very grateful to each of you for your honest interactions.

Contents

Section III: **IMPLICATIONS OF THE MODEL**

List of Figures

Chapter 1: **Presenting The 5 Stages**

Chapter 2: **Exit in Protestant missions**

Chapter 3: **Refining the model**

Chapter 4: **How long?**

Chapter 5: **Implications for mission agencies**

Chapter 6: **Sharing resources**

Foreword

If you think missionally you will like this book. It comes out of the mind and heart of a thoughtful, practical equipper. While the context of the 5 Stages is in cross cultural ministry, its concepts are applicable to any ministry anywhere.

I suspect the genesis of this book actually began in a family of rowdy, North Queensland boys. I'm told Lindsay and his brothers had a style that was in your face, make it happen, aggressive, quick witted and very practical. Linked to his formative years was his marriage to Rosalea Hotchkin who shares many of those characteristics herself but also brought to their shared lives her experiences as a missionary child in Papua New Guinea. Rosalea's parents were part of the first wave of missionaries in the Southern Highlands in the early 1960s introducing the gospel and guiding a church planting movement that continues to this day. Together, Lindsay and Rosalea planted a church in Cairns, Queensland before heading to Maputo, Mozambique to begin a ten-year ministry in Africa that included serving as Africa Area Director for Global Partners of The Wesleyan Church of North America. The genesis of this book comes out of a lifetime of hands on experience.

The world of missions is littered with evangelistic plans, programs and campaigns. Most of them were helpful in advancing Kingdom issues, but few of them fulfilled the promise with which they were launched. As a human enterprise, entrepreneurial leaders have devised ways to motivate and focus people. Before the end of the 19th and 20th Century's there were numerous strategies to complete the evangelization of humankind. I remember the positive influence Don McGavran's Church Growth writings had on me thirty years ago, but I also remember speaking to a group of mission executives about my weariness with the constant ministry "fads" that were imposed on field practitioners.

The leadership team of Global Partners wanted to explore what characteristics should be found in the churches that were emerging across the world. We wondered if we could develop a template that could guide our thinking and our ministry. Each of the leaders was invited to bring ideas. Lindsay's contribution developed into *The 5 Stages of Missions* which was adopted as our ministry template. We believe it provides a guide to develop a church from infancy to full missional maturity. We believe it raises the questions that need to be answered whether you are church planting in urban western cities or in a rural developing world community. We believe that it allows the natural, cultural expression of the gospel to flourish even as it helps to form and shape its organizational development. The *5 Stages* is not a program or a fad but a template to equip God's people to grow and develop the church to fruitfulness, maturity and mission.

I believe this book will stimulate you to think more deeply about the development and potential of ministry God has entrusted to you. I know it comes from a mind and heart that has been forged in spiritual discipline, biblical values and missional reality.

Don Bray
General Director of Global Partners 1992–2007.

Introduction

"This is a letter from the church in the Congo", the group leader said with a twinkle in his eye. He presented me with a magnificently crafted bronze hand holding a small bronze egg. "But", he continued, "You may not be able to read this letter, so I will tell you what it says. You hold the future of our small group in the palm of your hand. We have potential for life, but you must keep us warm and safe until we grow." I was serving as the Director for Global Partners for Africa at that time and the implications of receiving this gift were far-reaching.

It was a further two years before we finally held the inaugural national conference for these 4,000 believers in the south-east corner of the Democratic Republic of Congo. For those two years I struggled to find a gift to take in return; something suitable for such a celebration and something that spoke as eloquently as the bronze hand. I could not think of anything as clever as the gift I had received until I asked a Congolese friend for advice. In seconds he answered, "You must take them a drum." And I did!

I purchased the biggest drum that I could find and carried it through the borders to Lubumbashi for the conference. When the drum was presented to the conference this explanation was offered: "It takes two hands to play a drum. The international church is one hand and the Congolese church is the other hand. To really make music you need both hands playing together."

The 5 Stages of Missions describes the international partnership that we desire, and the steps involved in achieving the goal. The work of any mission agency is only complete when it has established a mature church, fully engaged in the work of international missions. The end result of missionary work is more complex than to simply *exit*, it is to establish an *international partnership* based on mutual respect and a common goal to reach the nations for Jesus Christ.

The gift of the bronze egg played a part in helping me to develop my own missiology. I pray that *The 5 Stages of Missions* will play some part in your ministry as you develop your own understanding of the issues and rewards in building healthy, multiplying new mission works.

Lindsay Cameron
Melbourne, Australia 2012.

Section I: **THE MODEL**

Chapter 1: **The 5 Stages of Missions**

Chapter 1: **Presenting The 5 Stages**

In past centuries Christian missionaries often went to countries where monotheism was a foreign concept and where provision of education, literacy and healthcare was minimal. The challenge of starting a new church was large and the time commitment was likely to include more than one generation of missionaries. In such cases, it would have been beneficial to the missionary team to have an overview of the strategy and goals of the mission. Unfortunately, strategies more often focused upon the task of initiating the missionary work, not upon a successful conclusion to the work. As the practices of colonialism fell into disrepute and as mission fields matured, agencies began to search more specifically for strategies for exiting the mission field. However, although mission agencies have learned much in this search, a commonly accepted overall strategy has not emerged. As a result, some mission efforts have lost direction.

The 5 Stages of Missions proposes five overall goals that face the mission agency, and that the progression through these *5 Stages* will mark the key role-changes that the missionary team negotiates during the course of a successful ministry. *The 5 Stages of Missions* encompasses the development of converts, disciples, pastors, leaders and partners in international ministry.

The 5 Stages of Missions process

Converts	Disciples	Pastors	Leaders	Partners

Winning converts to Jesus Christ is the initial purpose of the missionary presence. Once converts are won, every effort must be made to disciple every convert to become a mature follower of Jesus Christ; fully equipped for a victorious Christian life and able to represent Christ in his/her world. From those disciples a number will be trained to serve as pastors of local congregations. A few of those pastors, alongside a few mature lay-persons, will then emerge or be selected for further development to serve in denominational leadership and as bible college professors. Of that leadership pool, a small number will assume roles of international leadership and some of the disciples will be commissioned to go as missionaries to new fields.

First contacts

Stage 1 encompasses the period from the arrival of the first missionaries until a nucleus of converts has turned to Christ. This stage is characterized by an era when the missionaries are the primary evangelists. Missionary engagement in this stage assumes that the missionaries are not entering through a relationship with a pre-existing group of local believers, or that the pre-existing group does not have a complete doctrine or experience of salvation.

Some authors, such as Dr. Tom Steffen, have rightly pointed out that the work of missions starts with pre-entry preparation and with on-field pre-evangelism (Steffen, 1997: 6). Pre-evangelism might include a distinct phase of building credibility with the government or community and an extensive program of building relationships. However, these elements need not be a separate stage of missionary strategy; they belong under the first great missionary priority; that of making converts. Programs for preparation should be developed in greater detail by the individual agency according to its own ethos.

Stage 1: Making converts

Converts
First contacts: • Relationships • Evangelism • Ministries of compassion • Church planting

The stage of making converts can extend over quite a long period of time. It usually includes the work of language acquisition, cultural adaptation and the development of trust with the local community. In some situations, this stage can take decades. One example comes from Sierra Leone in West Africa where Wesleyan Methodist missionaries first arrived in 1889. It was 1919, thirty years later, before the first local church run by nationals was organized at Binkolo, with thirteen members (McLeister and Nicholson, 1976: 393). Even more poignant is the history of the mission at Kakuna in the far north of Sierra Leone amongst the staunchly Muslim, Susu tribe. This mission was started in 1939 by a Sierra Leonean church planter (Wesleyan Church of Sierra Leone, 1985: 9), and was supported by the presence of North American missionaries until 1969. In the late 1980s the mission station was finally turned over to the national church. Over that 50-year period, a former missionary reported one solitary Susu convert; the mission security watchman.

Stage 1 can include extreme deprivation for the missionary and sometimes it involves martyrdom. The veracity of the Gospel is proved through the witness of the missionary presence and through ministries of relief and development. In the case of the Wesleyan Methodist mission to Sierra Leone, eleven North Americans paid with their lives to establish this work. These pioneer missionaries are often seen as the heroes of missions, and rightly so. However, there is a danger when any one stage takes such an extended period of time: the mission can lose sight of the ultimate goals of indigenization and internationalization. Presence can become a goal in itself, and the missionaries can forget to progress on to the next stage.

Developing a presence and effective ministry in a new country has historically included ministries of relief and development, such as the development of schools and medical facilities. Although these facilities can continue to grow throughout the lifetime of the mission, their presence is listed as part of Stage 1 because alleviating urgent physical needs earns the missionaries the right to meet the community's spiritual needs. Caring for spiritual needs and for physical needs are the two faces of genuine Christian compassion. For this reason, it would not be appropriate to establish ministries of compassion as a separate stage of its own. Ministries of relief and development should always be part of the ongoing establishment and presence of the Church, and it should be a feature of the Church's ministry from Stage 1.

Teach believers

As soon as the first converts have responded to Christ, the work of discipleship becomes urgent. In fact, it is true to say that some discipleship commences prior to conversion. However, once the believer receives the Spirit a new ability to discern spiritual truth is granted (1 Corinthians 2: 14), and so, it is logical that discipleship cannot be completed until after conversion.

Stage 2: Making disciples

Disciples
Teach believers: • Teaching & preaching   • Consecration   • Small groups   • Literature

Of course, the missionaries will likely be heavily involved in the dual stages of evangelism and discipleship for some time. However, when the transition is made Stage 2 is characterized by the missionaries focused upon discipling believers so that the new converts take up the work of witnessing to the unchurched. This happens when a critical mass of converts is reached, and thereafter discipleship consumes the majority of missionary effort, which prepares a workforce of national evangelists. At this time the overall emphasis of the mission changes, although this does not deny that some team members may continue to exercise individual gifts of evangelism.

In Stage 2 the missionaries will have an increasing preaching load as the number of local churches increases. Disciples will be encouraged to experience a deeper walk with Christ through personal consecration and the infilling of the Holy Spirit. This stage will likely include some emphasis on small group ministry for the purpose of discipleship, and it may be marked by the printing of discipleship literature.

It could be argued that the work of Stage 2 will have a greater impact on the long-term success of the mission than any other single stage. It is at this formative time that new converts are taught the vital principles of witnessing, prayer, Bible reading, tithing, worship and ownership of the local church ministry. Furthermore, if the theology of the mission agency anticipates a deeper experience of consecration, baptism of the Spirit, sanctification, confirmation, victory, or even prosperity, this is the period when new believers are taught what to expect from their Christian faith. It is important that the mission has a strategy to disciple immediately and vigorously. There is a window of influence during which time the missionary "parents" are expected to guide new believers in the ways of the Faith. Insipid teaching or generic publications will hinder the development of the church for decades if an unconvincing effort is made in Stage 2.

As the number of local churches grows and the need for local pastors increases the work naturally progresses to Stage 3.

Prepare pastors

Stage 3 is when the missionaries establish a program to train some of the disciples to serve as pastors. This may be done through Theological Education by Extension (TEE) or in a residential program for pastoral training. This stage is characterized by the missionaries commencing and leading a pastoral training program, and by national workers taking on more of the pastoral role in the local churches. This stage will also likely include a standard for ordination to mark when a trainee has completed the requisite study and service.

Stage 3: Making pastors

Pastors

Prepare pastors:

- TEE
- Bible schools
- Ordination
- Emerging leaders

Stage 3 will be marked by the growing recognition of some key national workers as leaders. Ideally, these men and women demonstrate faithfulness and fruitfulness, and they have a growing influence among the churches. In some cases, the emerging leaders are chosen by the missionaries for other reasons, such as their submission to missionary management or because of personal loyalty. It is hard to describe any good long-term result from missionary-manipulated promotions. National workers who do not have an anointing for leadership from within the national church will forever struggle under the mantle of “missionary favorite”. Furthermore, the seeds of future division are planted when those with genuine gifts are frustrated by inferior leadership.

As emerging leaders develop they will likely begin to challenge the assumption of missionary leadership. Until this time the missionaries have been multiplying the ministry while essentially retaining control. It is at the transition between Stages 3 and 4 that the mission is most vulnerable to failure because it is precisely here that real power is relinquished.

Replace & redeploy

Stage 4 is when the missionaries undertake the task of replacing themselves. During this stage national workers are educated to equivalent levels as the missionaries, including post-graduate theological degrees, so that they can take over the tasks of bible college teaching and national church leadership. This stage is characterized by national workers leading the church within the boundaries of their own country. It necessarily means that missionaries begin to move out of leadership and some teaching positions, being replaced by trained national church workers. It usually means a declining number of missionaries on the field.

This is the most difficult stage for any mission. The first three stages are intuitive and comfortable. It is natural to make converts, disciple them and train some to be pastors. During this process the missionary retains field leadership and ensures that the work develops according to mission policy. The difficulty comes when it is time for the missionaries to release control of field leadership. This is both counter-intuitive and uncomfortable. This is when a *"5 Stages"* type of vision is essential to remind missionaries that the goal of indigenization is more important than the urge to control the details of the ministry. If indigenization only meant delegation of tasks, then it would be readily accomplished, but it does not. Indigenization must involve the release of real authority. Furthermore, it usually involves retiring some missionaries.

Stage 4: Making leaders

Leaders

Replace & redeploy:

- Nationals to post-grad level
- Re-assign expatriates
- Economic empowerment

These two hurdles to indigenization (release of authority and repatriation of missionaries) deserve further consideration, but for now the attitudes that cause failure in Stage 4 could be summarized simply in the following two fatal errors:

1) The mission is willing to release authority... as long as the national church continues to make decisions which have the mission's approval, and

2) The missionaries agree to the reduction in the number of missionary personnel... as long as the field waits upon natural retirement.

In the transition to Stage 4, these two destructive obstacles become the intuitive mission response that can hold up indigenization for decades.

In many mission field situations, graduate and post-graduate studies are not readily available. Furthermore, the pursuit of academic degrees is sometimes viewed as the imposition of a Western worldview which might seem inappropriate to the cultural need within the country. However, the discussion about higher education affords us an opportunity to examine what is the ultimate goal of the mission.

If the goal was simply an indigenous church; one that is equipped to carry the Gospel deeper into its own culture, then perhaps an international standard of formal education is not necessary. However, even this idea begs debate since the national church is never going to take over the training of national workers in the deeper truths of the faith unless some nationals have studied at a higher level. The alternative is that the mission agency simply continues to send in missionaries to provide the pastoral training, which is not indigenization at all. This would be similar to suspending your children's growth at 15 years old, when they are strong enough to plough the field but not ready to discuss farm finances with the bank manager. If the church is to be truly indigenous, then all aspects of church life should have national workers at their core. The church may supplement the work with international workers, but the backbone has to be national. If national staff is to form the backbone of the bible colleges, then they will require the same levels of education as is expected from missionaries.

If, however, the ultimate goal is to raise up international church leaders, international missionaries and partners in the work of international missions, then higher level theological education is essential. It is extremely difficult for any person to engage in the international arena as a genuine peer with those who have a significantly better education. Even when the national leader has a higher degree in a secular discipline, he or she cannot assume a leadership role in issues of theology and church administration without relevant credentials. Furthermore, even if the national worker is accepted as a peer, it will be even more difficult to rise to a role of international leadership over those who are better educated than oneself. It is difficult enough for a third-world leader to have to overcome financial and linguistic barriers. Education is one of the few truly achievable equalizers, and as such, it should be a priority for church leaders, even if only for their own self-confidence.

The approach taken to the issue of higher education will test whether Stage 5: partnership in international ministry is truly at the heart of the mission's goals or whether domestic management is the limit of the vision.

International ministry

Stage 5 is achieved when the national church accepts its responsibility as a mature unit of the international church. This maturity is characterized by international involvement in leadership and missions. A mature church in any culture should be motivated toward mission outreach into new tribal or ethnic groups within their country and to countries beyond their own borders. If the national church does not have a desire for outreach, then the Gospel of a redemptive God has not properly been received. Representatives of the mature church should take their place alongside other international leaders in denominational and interdenominational forums. Maturity is to become fully engaged in the Great Commission.

Experience suggests that national church leaders are often ready to assume roles of international leadership ahead of their capacity to carry such a financial obligation. This is a real hindrance, for it is difficult to function as a peer to other international leaders when your travel budget is still governed by the charity of others.

Stage 5: Making international partners

Partners

International ministry:

- Missions to other cultures
- Missions to other nations
- International leaders

A second significant factor in Stage 5 is whether the originating mission agency is able or willing to allow national leaders to exercise true international leadership. An irony of missions is that sometimes missions can have at its roots an attitude of superiority and charity. It is not so unusual to hear of missionaries who are motivated by a sense of pity for people of a different race and color. If this pity arises out of their own unshakable sense of ethnocentric superiority, rather than from humble and grateful submission to God, then the missionary lives with an abiding assurance that these people will never be able to govern themselves adequately.

Sadly, sometimes it is not giftedness and anointing that are used to assess leadership qualifications. Issues of cultural superiority and respect for education and prosperity too readily determine who is eligible for leadership. Often the most spiritually mature leaders live in deep dependence upon Christ in physical deprivation and suffering or under persecution and oppression. Yet, these giants of the faith are passed over because they do not have the financial resources or academic qualifications necessary for the prestige of international leadership. This is a great loss to the Church. These men and women have often experienced aspects of walking with Jesus far beyond the experience of others who are more regularly called upon to preach at international conventions. If the original sending church is not willing to set aside its own cultural prejudices, then the greatest impediment to achieving Stage 5 maturity may come from within the mission agency or its controlling body.

The thesis of this work is that successful missions must address the *5 Stages* of development. These stages may be slow in coming, they may be hindered by political and social conditions and they may even meet resistance from the originating mission body, but they remain the goal at the heart of Christianity. The challenge of Jesus Christ to "go and make disciples of all nations" is a claim upon true believers of all nations. Consequently, a mission work is not complete until the new national church accepts its responsibility to reach the world for Christ.

The *5 Stages* model lays out the different phases of the developing ministry in a systematic way. These stages are described in chronological order, although, even in traditional missions the logical progression is not always sequential. For example, a significant element of Stage 5 is the development of second generation missions; when the mission field becomes a missionary sending agency. However, clearly, a vision for missions should be fostered from the time of early discipleship. The Gospel is for sharing! In this way, Stage 5 has origins in Stages 1 and 2. Furthermore, it is normal for missionary activity to span several stages of development at any given time as it disengages from one task and engages in another. Consequently, the ordering of the *5 Stages* sequentially is a helpful educational tool but should not be applied too rigidly.

The bullet points given to illustrate the ministries that occur at each stage are not intended to be prescriptive either. Clearly there are many exceptions to these sub-points. Literature may be a feature of evangelism and pastoral training, not just a feature of discipleship. Ministries of compassion should be evident at all stages as an expression of true Christian care. Outreach to other cultures often occurs as a natural part of Stage 2; not waiting for Stage 5.

In its simplest form, *The 5 Stages of Missions* highlights the simple truth that missions encompasses the development of converts, disciples and pastors, leading to a nationalized church, and finally to partnership in international ministry.

In many situations today, ministry is joined alongside existing fellowships or in countries where higher educational and health standards exist. In these cases, ministry may not be entered at Stage 1; it may be entered at a different developmental phase, with different priorities and methods. However, the global perspective afforded by *The 5 Stages of Missions* is still relevant as it then facilitates more accurate assessment and development of forward strategy, and will keep the team focused upon the goal of developing full partners in the work of outreach to the whole world.

The 5 Stages of Missions model (App. A)

Converts	*Disciples*	*Pastors*	*Leaders*	*Partners*
First contacts: • Relationships • Evangelism • Ministries of compassion • Church planting	*Teach believers:* • Teaching & preaching • Consecration • Small groups • Literature	*Prepare pastors:* • TEE • Bible schools • Ordination • Emerging leaders	*Replace & redeploy:* • Nationals to post-grad level • Re-assign expatriates • Economic empowerment	*International ministry:* • Missions to other cultures • Missions to other nations • International leaders

Section II: **ORIGINS OF THE MODEL**

Chapter 2: **Exit in Protestant missions**

Chapter 3: **Refining the model**

Chapter 2: **Exit in Protestant missions**

The Christian Church has been engaged in missions since Jesus Christ commissioned the early church to "go and make disciples of all nations" (Matthew 28: 19). In fact, two thousand years before Christ, Abraham was commissioned and promised that "all peoples on earth will be blessed through you" (Genesis 12: 3). The Apostle Paul was set apart and commissioned by God to preach Jesus Christ among the Gentiles. Patrick was called of God to reach Ireland; Boniface, to reach the German tribes. Ignatius was directed to Europe and Xavier to India, the East Indies and Japan.

However, once missionaries overcame the enormous hurdles of reaching the field and initiating an indigenous church, they regularly found the task of leaving to be, oddly, more difficult than arriving. While the development of an effective exit strategy is a topic that often engages the minds of those who are involved in the work of Christian missions, it has proven hard to implement on many fields. It is worthwhile to track the ebb and flow of thinking in this subject of an exit strategy. It was with the dawn of the Modern Missions Era, in the afterglow of the Great Awakening of Great Britain, that the theory of missions began to be formulated for the Protestant Church.

In the eighteenth-century Jonathan Edwards, John Wesley, George Whitfield, Howell Harris and others were powerfully used of God in the evangelical awakening that swept across the British Isles and America. Evangelical faith made claim to a personal relationship with Christ, assurance of salvation and holiness of heart. It was natural that this promise of personal faith would soon inspire believers to reach out to peoples of other nations. The trickle of missionary efforts evident in the eighteenth century became a flood in the nineteenth. Numerous mission societies were born, and thousands heeded the call to preach Jesus Christ in foreign lands in what is said to have been the real beginning of Protestant missions (LaTourette, 1999: 1,033).

The heroes of this era are represented by a few outstanding names; William Carey in India, David Livingstone in Africa and Hudson Taylor in China. These missionaries of the early nineteenth century shaped the practice of Protestant missions. At the same time, however, other names have endured as those who shaped the theory of missions. None made more impact than Henry Venn and Rufus Anderson. The theory of these two mission agency executives continues to be a cornerstone of mission theory today. They sought to articulate and encourage the indigenization of national churches. Indigenization of the national church is the larger work that incorporates the task of missionary exit.

Henry Venn and Rufus Anderson

Henry Venn (1796–1873) served as leading secretary of the Church Missionary Society (Anglican) from 1841–72 and Rufus Anderson (1796–1880) served as senior secretary of the American Board of Commissioners for Foreign Missions from 1832–66. Although these two contemporaries served in different parts of the world, they are often listed together because of the work that they did in formalizing the common thinking on missions at that time.

They are credited with recording the *indigenous church* principle or the *Three-Selfs* concept; i.e. the mission field should be self-supporting, self-governing, and self-propagating. These concepts are not believed to have originated with either Venn or Anderson, but these men are acknowledged as those responsible for articulating the growing awareness of their time in a way that endures as a cornerstone for mission theory until this day (Shenk, 1990: 28). The *Three-Selfs* concept is a powerful example of how a simple truth stated in a concise manner has lasting impact.

Rufus Anderson believed that "missions are instituted for the spread of a scriptural, self-propagating Christianity. This is their only aim." This aim is achieved through four phases: "(1) the conversion of lost men, (2) organizing them into churches, (3) giving these churches a competent native ministry, and (4) conducting them to the stage of independence and (in most cases) self-propagation" (Rufus Anderson in Beaver, 1979: 94).

Anderson's strategy of missions

	Anderson
1	Conversion
2	Local churches
3	Native ministry
4	Independence

Henry Venn, on the other hand, had more to say about a distinct exit strategy. He described a mature church as one which was self-reliant, with an effective mission program. The original missionary work was to be "scaffolding" while the church was the "edifice". Venn coined the phrase, "the euthanasia of a mission." He taught that the "formal mission structure was an abnormality to be removed as early as expedient, and that the true calling of a mission was to be engaged in continuous advance into the 'regions beyond'"(Venn as quoted in Shenk, 1977b: 18). "The goal must be to maintain continuous advance in mission. Do not wait to fully evangelize 'Jerusalem' before moving on" (Venn as quoted in Shenk, 1977a: 475). Venn believed that a successful exit, not too early and not too late, was the crown of the mission enterprise.

Venn had a strong interest in the economic development of the national church. He believed that "if people's economic needs were met through constructive and legitimate commerce, evils such as slavery would be eliminated" (Shenk, 1977b: 17). This commitment to economic development is a necessary provision if the national church is to become self-supporting.

Clearly Rufus Anderson and Henry Venn were men of their time. Their views were shaped by the thinking and the events of the era in which they lived. Their views reflected and focused a growing consensus among mission workers. Over time their strategies have been sifted, and while some strategies have fallen into disrepute, their *Three-Selfs* emphasis has continued to serve as a focal point for indigenization of the national church.

In response to Anderson and Venn, three points are noteworthy.

1) After 200 years of mission experience, clearly articulated steps toward exit are past due. Principles are often intuitively discovered in the mission community before they are articulated and recorded. This appears to have been so with the *Three-Selfs*. This is good, in as much as it provides some testing for theories before they are propagated as truth. However, if the principles are not clearly articulated once tested, the advantage is lost; for surely it means that new missionaries are less likely to be confronted with this wisdom until they too have experience on the field. A model to guide missionaries to achieve indigenization is one such opportunity lost.

2) Whilst it is encouraging to see that *exit* was so strongly emphasized by Henry Venn two centuries ago, it is saddening to realize that this call was somehow muted. Time has shown that the primacy of the mission station and the ongoing indispensable role of the missionary have crippled the national church. "The longer Venn observed missions, the more critical he became of missionary paternalism and domination" (Shenk, 1990: 29).

3) Venn's emphasis on commerce is encouraging. As will be seen later in this study, economic empowerment continues to be a gap in exit strategies today.

A striking enigma about Anderson and Venn, these two men who have so profoundly influenced modern mission thought, is that neither of them served as foreign missionaries themselves. Anderson's 44 years of ministry were spent as an administrator in North America (Beaver, 1979: 94). Venn, likewise, never served as a missionary, and even more strangely, he is believed to have never visited the overseas' work (Shenk, 1977b: 19). Nonetheless, time has proven the thinking of both men to be solid. This lends credence to the thought that both men were simply formalizing the missiological thinking of their time, and perhaps it points to the conclusion that those who are serving on the field, intimately entwined in local ministries, emotions and personalities, are not always the best ones to formulate objective mission policy.

John Nevius

John Nevius (1829–93) was a missionary influenced by the concept of a self-supporting, self-governing, and self-propagating indigenous church. As a Presbyterian missionary to China, sent in 1854, he sought to break away from the effects of the old methodology whereby mission agencies paid the salaries of local workers. He taught that local congregations should support their own outreach efforts. Nevius took this emphasis to Korea when he visited there in 1890 and his teaching greatly impacted the growth of the Korean Church.

Nevius established a "volunteer, unpaid corps of national evangelists who would be trained by rigorous Bible study and practical experience" (Matthews, 1990: 300). His ministry illustrates the potency of a clearly articulated strategy. He caught the *Three-Selfs* vision and devoted his life to implementing it. However, a clearly articulated strategy can also draw criticisms into the open. Toward the end of the nineteenth century, as the mission agencies began to comprehend the implications of this radical break from paternalism, the *Three-Selfs* concept came under attack.

Mission agencies and missionaries questioned whether national churches could properly govern themselves. Eventually a solution was proposed by German missiologist, Gustav Warneck, that national churches should "remain under the supervision of the missionary until full ecclesiastical development had been attained" (Matthews, 1990: 300).

This illustrates a sad truth about human nature and mission work: many would agree that a self-governing church is the goal but would also hold reservations about the national worker's ability to govern properly. In fact, the ethnocentric tendency draws the missionary to the conclusion that the work is never done properly unless it is done to the missionary's satisfaction. How else was Warneck's *full ecclesiastical development* to be interpreted?

Rolland Allen

Rolland Allen (1868–1947) might be described as a man born outside his time, or perhaps as a prophet calling the mission community back to a neglected task. Allen served with the (Anglican) Society for the Propagation of the Gospel in China. His writings represented an escalation in the call for an early exit from the mission field.

In the earlier of Allen's two influential missiological works, *Missionary Methods—St. Paul's or Ours?* first published in 1912, Allen drew attention to the rapid exit that Paul affected in his missionary work. In his later book, *The Spontaneous Expansion of the Church*, first published in 1927, Allen expanded upon the example of Paul's ministry by showing that the Holy Spirit is able to lead the infant national church toward maturity without ongoing missionary help. The later book, generally speaking, is an application of the earlier book.

Allen maintained that the task before the Apostle Paul was not so different to the task before modern missionaries. He argues that Paul's advantage was quite minimal (Allen, 1998: 22). Missionaries should adopt strategies similar to Paul's and should be able to exit in a short period of time. He goes on to argue that the underlying reason that modern missionaries do not exit sooner is because they do not trust the national worker and they do not trust the power and presence of the Holy Spirit (Allen, 1997: 36).

Allen concludes by offering the advice that once the missionaries have baptized some new converts, 1) they must teach the fundamentals of Christianity—the creed, 2) they must teach reliance upon the Bible—the Gospel, 3) they must pass over authority to administer the sacraments, 4) they must ordain local workers, and 5) they must teach the necessity of evangelism and missions. After this, they should withdraw from the new work, but not neglect it. The ongoing missionary obligation is to provide for education (Allen, 1997: 147–51).

In responding to Allen's work, it is necessary to remember the missiological climate in which he ministered. In the middle of the 1800s there had been profound strategic advances articulated by Anderson and Venn in the area of indigenization of the national church. Some missionaries began to implement these theories in extreme measure, as illustrated by Nevius. However, the colonial need to patronize and keep control worked against this new emphasis, and the pendulum of mission strategy swung back toward a paternalistic mind-set by the late 1800s. Allen entered the debate in the early 1900s, and vigorously refuted the paternalistic bent. For this he is to be applauded.

Allen's strategy in contrast to Anderson

	Anderson	Allen
1	Conversion	Conversion and baptism
2	Local churches	Disciple new converts
3	Native ministry	Sacraments, ordination, missions
4	Independence	Withdraw, monitor education

Unfortunately, Rolland Allen's extreme views on replicating the ministry of the Apostle Paul undermined the influence of his writing. This is such a central and oft quoted concept that we shall look closer at these issues in a later chapter.

Two wars and the ecumenical movement

The framework provided by Anderson and Venn remained the reference point for mission theory into the twentieth century, even when mission practice contradicted the goal of the *Three-Selfs* indigenous church. Despite the call from Venn to euthanize the mission, political colonialism and mission practice appeared to be inseparable. Ethnocentric paternalism and perceived Western superiority distorted logic in mission strategy.

However, in the approach to the twentieth century new priorities began to stir the mission community. The violent rending of old-world values caused by two world wars propelled missions into a new era. The priority that was stirring the mission community was the desire for cooperation between the numerous mission agencies now active. "William Carey proposed an international conference in 1810, and in 1888 the German historian of missions, Gustav Warneck, proposed an international missionary conference to be held every 10 years" (Fuller, 1981: 46). Throughout the nineteenth century a growing number of mission agencies and national churches began to hold regional conferences for the purpose of cooperation. These became especially evident in India beginning in 1825, in Japan in 1872 and in China in 1877. The following years saw joint missionary conferences in Mexico and South Africa, and for the Muslim world.

Meanwhile, sending countries also began to hold cooperative conferences – in England, Germany, Holland, and North America. These stirrings of cooperation climaxed when more than 1,200 members of mission agencies from all over the world met at the World Missionary Conference, held in Edinburgh in 1910. This meeting is a "landmark in the history of the Ecumenical Movement" (LaTourette, 1999: 1,334). It led to the formation of the International Missionary Council (IMC) in 1921, after the First World War. The IMC ran concurrently with the World Missionary Conference until the IMC was absorbed into the World Council of Churches in 1961.

World War I and World War II struck at the heart of established Christendom, especially for the Protestant Church. Germany was the homeland of Protestantism, and Germany was to be humbled and reshaped. A large part of Protestant Germany was divided off and came under the communist rule of Russia. Furthermore, millions of German Protestants were displaced by the realignment of Poland's border with Germany. Confidence in the superiority of the Christian faith took a blow, and colonialism itself fell out of favor. Venn's call for "euthanasia of the mission" was propelled forward by anti-colonial sentiment (Shenk, 1996: 34–35).

The stress and fracturing that these events caused the Protestant Church weakened some through disillusionment and strengthened others through the re-evaluation of former values and through new growth. The Ecumenical Movement grew rapidly during the period, and again missions played a significant role. Once World War II commenced in Europe in 1939, German missionaries were stranded, cut off from their German support base. In 1940, because of German occupation, missionaries from France, Belgium, the Netherlands, Denmark and Norway were also cut off from their support base. The IMC organized the Orphaned Missions Fund to draw support from other countries for these stranded missionaries. As a result, according to the IMC records, "not a single unit of the Continental missionary enterprises was suspended because of lack of funds" (LaTourette, 1999: 1,378).

Missions provided a platform upon which otherwise divided denominations could agree. The urgency of missions and the harshness of the mission field had done much to pare away traditional denominational antagonism. Differences seem less significant on the mission field. So, just as missions had been a catalyst for the emergence of the Ecumenical Movement, missions was instrumental in bringing it to maturity. The World Council of Churches began to function in 1938 and, after World War II, was officially constituted in Amsterdam in 1948. However, the partnership between missions and ecumenicalism was a two-way affair. Missions, in its simplicity, provided a less threatening arena for inter-church cooperation, but in return, missions became the testing grounds for theological debate. Once the ecumenical movement assumed responsibility for the work of missions, the discussion would no longer be simply about Venn's ideas of the indigenized church. The missions debate now included discussion on the place of social development in missions, the question of Christ's unique role in salvation, and the hastening of Christ's return by preaching to all nations.

The envelopment of the IMC by the World Council of Churches was as rapid as it was inevitable.

- 1910—The World Missionary Conference in Edinburgh set the priority of evangelization.
- 1921—Following World War I, the IMC was established.
- 1928—By the time of the second World Missionary Conference, held in Jerusalem, the world had changed in fundamental ways. The futile bloodshed of World War I and the subsequent disillusionment played an important part in eroding Christian convictions. The Church was showing an increasing desire to focus on their role at home, not just on the foreign fields. Liberal theology and Universalism began to challenge the idea that Jesus Christ is the unique Savior. In Jerusalem, the secretary from the IMC "personally circulated a book, *Reality*, which questioned the deity of Jesus" (Fuller, 1981: 47).
- 1938—When the third World Missionary Conference was held in Madras, the emphasis had shifted away from *evangelization* to *the church*. Missions was to be

viewed as one part of the ministry of the Church (Fuller, 1981: 47–48).

- 1948—The first World Council of Churches was assembled in Amsterdam and the ecumenical movement was officially launched.
- 1957—The IMC met in Accra, Ghana, at which time integration with the World Council of Churches was proposed. The merger was accomplished in 1961 in New Delhi.
- 1974—Some feel that the missionary priority has since been lost to the World Council of Churches. In fact, to some extent this shift was aided by the withdrawal and realignment of some mission agencies with other, more evangelical organizations. A landmark in this process was the formation of the Lausanne Committee for World Evangelization which developed from the International Congress on World Evangelization held in 1974 in Lausanne, Switzerland.

In this period surrounding the two World Wars, when old absolutes came under heavy fire, the very need for missionaries was questioned. As early as February 1971, John Gatu, General Secretary of the Presbyterian Church of East Africa proposed a five-year withdrawal of all missionary personnel. Later that same year, Gatu announced, "I will go further and say that missionaries should be withdrawn, period. The reason is that we must allow God the Holy Spirit to direct our next move without giving Him a timetable" (Gatu, as quoted in Fuller, 1981: 100).

This call for a moratorium of foreign missions was repeated at the Bangkok conference, and then was officially adopted in Lusaka in 1974 at the All Africa Conference of Churches (AACC).

It was later redefined by the AACC to be a call to action directed to the African church, rather than a call to cease action to the mission agencies (Fuller, 1981: 100–01). Nonetheless, the long association between colonialism and missions was now clearly to be tolerated no longer.

The development of mission strategy in the ecumenical movement is a polarized discussion. Various authors assert their own perspective about the merit or the corruption that ecumenism has caused. Regardless of this, what is clear is that the vision of Venn, Anderson, Nevius and Allen to establish a self-governing national church has been forcefully restated in the anti-colonial sentiment, especially through the extreme of the moratorium discussion. Subsequently, new authors have taken up the call for effective exit from a mission setting.

Donald McGavran

Donald McGavran, after a full career as a missionary in India with the United Christian Missionary Society, returned to the United States to champion the Church Growth Movement. This movement was primarily focused towards missions, later to be applied within the North American context by Win Arn. Missions added a new term to its vocabulary when the term *church planting* became synonymous with *mission*; thereby providing a way for missions to jettison some of the stigma of an old colonial practice.

Donald McGavran has been described as "the missiological giant of our generation" (McGavran, 1989: 344). He started the Institute of Church Growth in Oregon in 1961, and the School of World Missions at Fuller Theological Seminary in California in 1965. His use of the term *church growth* in reference to missions had great impact. The Great Commission had become synonymous with Church Growth.

> The conviction that the first essential of mission/church growth is to realize that God wants his lost children found and enfolded. Eternal God commands church growth. Jesus Christ gave his disciples the Great Commission, and the entire New Testament assumes that Christians, as a normal part of their lives, will proclaim Jesus Christ as God and Savior and encourage men and women to become his disciples and responsible members of his church (McGavran, 1986: 57).

A second element of McGavran's influence has been in his rebuttal of those who would seek to turn missions into a form of compassionate ministry without the element of evangelism. He refuted the concept, insisting that discipleship is the central task of missions (McGavran, 1986: 54).

Donald McGavran did much to draw his generation back to the essentials of missions and to rediscover the study of missions. However, there are two risks in over-emphasizing McGavran's teachings: there is a greater need for *exit* in missions than in domestic church planting, and community development is essential for *exit*.

Church planting in one's homeland has some fundamental differences to mission work in a foreign field. One of the greatest differences is in the expectation to exit. Church planters may, and often do, devote their whole lives to developing single churches. Missionaries who devote their whole lives to the development of one single ministry will likely have failed in the primary goal of raising up national church leaders and a self-propagating church.

While not debating McGavran's call for evangelism to remain at the heart of missions, the truth must be retained that community development is often an essential ingredient in establishing a self-sustaining national church. If people cannot read, how can they study the Bible? If people can't study the Bible, how can they grow in God's truths without a missionary presence? Literacy is essential to theological self-sustainability. It might also be argued that if an economic base is not established, the church cannot truly become financially self-sustaining.

C. Peter Wagner and W. Harold Fuller

C. Peter Wagner provides some insightful additions into the goals of missions, and therefore, into the study of *exit* in missions. He describes three signs of a mature church (Wagner, 1971: 163–67). These help in defining what characteristics a mature church should exhibit.

- Mature churches can take care of themselves. "A mature church is capable of solving its own problems, and developing its own characteristic life style."
- Mature churches serve the needs of others through social concern.
- Mature churches are relevant to their community. The church should not be out-of-touch because of ineffective communication (Wagner, 1971: 164).

Wagner defines the goals of missions through four phases of missionary work: "evangelization", "church development" (discipleship and indigenous leadership), "consultant", and exit when "the church launches a mission" of its own (Wagner,

1971: 176). These four phases readily compare to former strategists.

Wagner's strategy in contrast to Anderson and Allen

	Anderson	Allen	Wagner
1	Conversion	Conversion and baptism	Evangelism
2	Local churches	Disciple new converts	Church development
3	Native ministry	Sacraments, ordination, missions	Consultant to national church
4	Independence	Withdraw, monitor education	Exit at 2nd generation missions

Wagner offers some challenge to the Venn model of the indigenous church, and in a way, to the church planting movement of late twentieth century. He states that the goal of missions is not simply to plant autonomous churches internationally; it is to plant disciples (Wagner, 1971: 168).

This work offers some fresh thought in the strategy of missions. His four phases of missions are especially relevant to our current study. However, there are some points that beg further discussion: the phase of *church development* is too broad, the phase of *consultant* is not explained, and the phase of *exit* is not developed.

Phase two, the *church development* phase, appears to incorporate the entire process from discipleship through to the establishment of fully equipped national leadership. Experience would suggest that this is the major portion of the entire process, and deserves more attention than Wagner's outline provides, if these stages are to serve as a guide to missionary practice.

Phase three, the *consultant* phase is quite hard to define. Wagner explains that this is not the time for *exit*. Missionaries may remain under a variety of structural arrangements. However, Wagner does not explain what their purpose is during that time. It could be that the missionaries stay around with no responsibility for the running of the church, but with many opinions. This is the phase at which Wagner's model appears to be most dangerous.

Finally, in phase four, Wagner describes the time when the national church has matured to the point of running its own mission program. He gives the helpful admonition that the development of second-generation missions is too often neglected. At that time the original mission exits. However, this raises more questions than it answers: Must the mission leave? Cannot the mission provide expertise in the development of the new second-generation mission? Is there no ongoing relationship between the mission and the national church?

W. Harold Fuller, in his excellent work on the church-mission relationship, takes C. Peter Wagner's four phases of missionary work, and makes some helpful additions (Fuller, 1981: 127).

- Phase one (evangelism), Fuller titles *Pioneer*. At this stage the missionary provides leadership and does the ministry.
- Phase two (church development), Fuller titles *Parent*. He describes a period when the mission is providing teaching without paternalism.
- Phase three (consultant), Fuller titles *Partner*. Here the national church cares for its own internal matters.

> Unfortunately, Fuller does not make any more progress in explaining what the missionary's work actually is during this phase.

Phase four (mission), Fuller titles *Participant*. This is a helpful expansion of Wagner's model. Fuller allows that the mission may remain, but "as long as the mission remains, it should use its gifts to strengthen the church" (Fuller, 1981: 272). He also allows that the mission should have moved onto other missions elsewhere.

This work of Fuller's is very helpful, though it still does not fully answer the questions raised in our survey of Wagner's original model.

Tom Steffen

Tom Steffen served with New Tribes Mission from 1969 to 1989 in the Philippines before taking a teaching role in missions at Biola University in California. Steffen's own dissatisfaction with current policy on the mission field led him to a clear emphasis on *Phase-out*, or, on the exit strategy. In this emphasis, Steffen provides the clearest attempt to address the issue of *exit* thus far.

The problems that he worked through are problems that many missionaries face. Clearly though, Steffen's ability to articulate the issues has led him further than most in proposing a model to resolve the issues of staying indefinitely on the mission field (Steffen, 1997: 3).

Steffen proposed five stages of phase-out:

(a) Pre-entry,

(b) Pre-evangelism,
(c) Evangelism,
(d) Post-evangelism,
(e) Phase-out (Steffen, 1997: 6).

A core element in Steffen's proposal is in his definition of phase-out "as programmed absences by the church planters that encourage nationals to take up their rightful responsibilities as leaders and multipliers of the church planting movement" (Steffen, 1997: 9).

Steffen's strategy in contrast to Anderson and Allen

	Anderson	**Allen**	**Steffen**
-1			Pre-entry
1	Conversion	Conversion and baptism	Pre-evangelism & evangelism
2	Local churches	Disciple new converts	Post-evangelism
3	Native ministry	Sacraments, ordination, missions	Phase-out – programmed absences
4	Independence	Withdraw, monitor education	

This work by Steffen is a refreshing new look at missions that calls for a long-term strategy to develop competent national leadership. It is an invaluable resource to missiologists, and perhaps the clearest outline available to the purposes of this study. However, there exists a fundamental difference between the focus of Steffen's work and *The 5 Stages of Missions*.

Steffen's focus is on phasing out the missionary venture. The goal of the *5 Stages* is on developing the national leaders toward partnership in the international work. *Phase-out*, and even the term used thus far in this study, *exit*, can have the implication that there comes a time of separation, and that this is a goal in itself. The growing argument of this study is that the handing over of responsibility to the national leadership is just one more step in the process of abiding and maturing relationship, from parent to peer. It should not imply ultimate separation. In maturity, both the mission field and the international church work together to partner in the work of reaching the globe for Christ.

It must be noted that Steffen is not against this goal of international partnership in any way, and in fact, he speaks about "maintaining relationships" after phase-out (Steffen, 1997: 19). However; there is a need for a more deliberate statement that internationalization is the final goal. Phasing-out is just one step toward that goal. The ultimate challenge comes when the mission agency is required to accept the national leaders as real peers; genuine equals in the work of evangelizing the world.

In Steffen's model he does not quite finish the transition to international leadership. He is still describing the missionary as the resident advisor in the final stage of phase-out. In this, Wagner can be commended for going further in the process to the establishment of second-generation missions. However, the *5 Stages* model goes further again, describing a situation where the missionary might become the learner and the international leader might be accepted as the expert. The international leader may even be invited to come to the mission agency's country to speak as an advisor on church growth or evangelism. The final stage of missions can be ministry reflected back upon the sending agency itself, when the mission agency breaks free from unconscious notions of superiority and is able to accept international brothers and sisters as equals, and even as authorities.

Other recent contributors

In recent literature there appears to be a growing call for a strategic plan of exit by mission agencies. Hans Finzel describes his experience of *exit* after 3 years in East Germany. He asks, "Why was I saying good-bye? Why were we pulling out? Because we had failed? No—the opposite, because we were successfully done!" (Finzel, 1992: 103). It would be misleading to conclude that Finzel had accomplished the broad range of missionary objectives in his brief three-year term of missionary service, but nonetheless, this article is an example of a growing awareness of the need to exit.

Finzel's model is also valuable because it exposes a growing awareness of the issue of internationalization and because Finzel draws a helpful distinction between *exit* and *closure*; *closure* does not exclude ongoing partnership (Fox, 2001: 303).

Finzel's strategy in contrast to Anderson and Steffen

	Anderson	**Steffen**	***Finzel***
-1		Pre-entry	
1	Conversion	Pre-evangelism & Evangelism	Initial entry
2	Local churches	Post-evangelism	First fruits
3	Native Ministry	Phase-out – Programmed absences	-National leaders -Partnership -National control
4	Independence		Complete nationalization
5			Global networking

The emphasis on the need for an exit strategy is not new; nor is it a radical new insight. However, it is clear that after 2,000 years of mission work, far more effort has been put into the practice of missions than the theory of missions, and within that limited theory, more emphasis has been put into *entry* than into *exit*. There is a need for a clear and complete model for the mission endeavor, from entry to exit, that will better prepare the missionary by outlining the long-term goal to those who may become engrossed in the immediate task. A statement published in 1994, "We desperately need a new model for evaluating missionary effectiveness and worth" (Monsma), is shocking, not because it says something new but because it describes a need so long unsatisfied.

There are many who have served before us with a clear strategy of mission. Their experience and wisdom aids in defining what the distinct stages of the missionary task should be. When we define the task of mission work, then we can determine how and when to exit.

In 2004, Dr. Wayne Wright, a former General Director for Global Partners, shared an outline given to him in 1951 by veteran missionary, Flora Belle Slater (personal communication). Ms. Slater had captured the vision of former missionaries with the simple outline:

GET IN
GET AHEAD
GET BESIDE
GET BEHIND
GET OUT

The emphasis on missionary exit is not a new study. It is a subject that has drawn the thoughts of many who have served in missions. However, the lack of conclusion to this matter is troubling. Perhaps it has simply taken the church this many years to break free from a colonial mind-set and accept that the mission field can truly become an international peer.

Chapter 3: **Refining the model**

I first presented *The 5 Stages of Missions* model to the leadership team of Global Partners[1] in Indianapolis in 2002. Through interaction with this team and with field leadership, the model has been refined and the focus of the final stages has been clarified. Describing this process is the simplest way to explain the growing conviction that international partnership is the truest test of maturity for both the mission field and the mission agency.

For a number of years there had been a growing discussion amongst Global Partners' leadership on the need to establish a policy for exiting the older mission fields. This was especially felt necessary for the fields in Africa, South America and the Pacific where many fields had been started a century ago. This discussion had been given life when the former Soviet Union collapsed, and dramatic new mission opportunities opened up across the former USSR, including Russia and eastern Europe. The awareness was further increased by a growing emphasis on creative access into Muslim countries; that is, using trade and development ministries as an entry strategy, rather than overt mission work. This Muslim emphasis was catapulted forward with the 9/11 attack on the World Trade Center buildings in New York in 2001. With so many new opportunities

---

[1] Global Partners is the mission department of the Wesleyan Church of North America.

for missions in Asia and Europe, the question of when we would be released from Africa, Latin America and the Pacific became urgent.

The practical question which started out as, "At what stage have we finished our task in long-standing mission fields?" developed to include the question, "What will our ongoing partnership with mature fields involve?" Early discussions centered on development of contracts for missionaries that called for redeployment at the completion of specific tasks. In time the discussions moved on to include the development of an International Conference in which the North American church would be just one voice amidst a spectrum of mature international churches.

Africa has the oldest of the Global Partners' mission fields, and yet, it still has some of the most dependent fields. Therefore, this discussion about exit strategies was of vital interest to Africa, and to me, since I was serving as the Africa Area Director. Furthermore, in Africa, Global Partners has primarily focused on the English and Portuguese speaking countries, where traditional African religions had been encountered. We had done very little to reach into the majority of the African countries: those with French and Arabic language and Muslim religion. Therefore, the refocusing toward Muslim countries in the Middle East also prompted the discussion that was long overdue and of vital importance to the African work—what of the Islamic majority in Africa?

Review by missionary leadership

The 2002 meeting responded enthusiastically to *The 5 Stages of Missions* model reinforcing some concepts and offering some additional insights.

- The development of hospitals and schools in the evangelistic ministries should be viewed as part of a larger commitment to Christ through ministries of compassion.

- The commitment to missions found in the *Partners* stage, must be introduced to the national church much earlier in the field development if there is to be a sense of *mission* present in the final stage.

- The model is going to generate fear in the mission fields because of the implication that the international relationship would be severed after Stage 5. This concern was especially expressed on behalf of the Latin American fields.

- The model could be expanded to show at what stage local churches are organized into districts, and at what stage a national structure is formalized.

One other observation that came from the Leadership Council was that *The 5 Stages of Missions* describes a circular goal. It starts out with missionary work and culminates in missionary work. The following model illustrates this point.

The 5 Stages as a circular goal

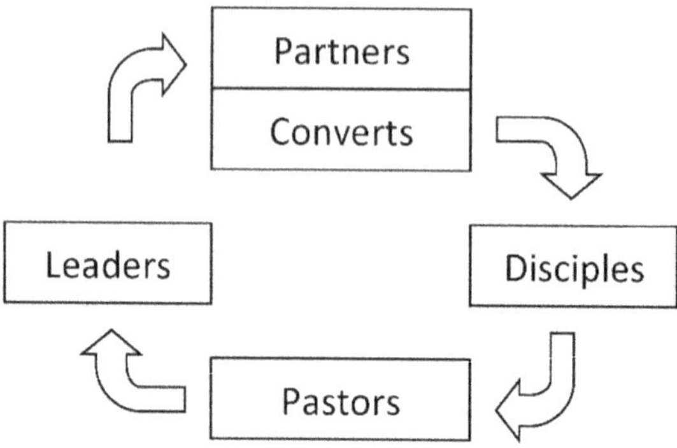

Later the same year I took the model back to the Leadership Council with some substantial applications. These can be grouped into two emphases:

- *The 5 Stages of Missions* model can be used as a diagnostic tool, to evaluate the development of a mission field.

- *The 5 Stages of Missions* model illustrates the need for decreasing missionary leadership at stages of increasing national leadership.

The model could be presented to field leadership, either missionary or national workers, to rate the successful completion of each component. At the completion of the assessment, this evaluation could then be used to place a national church predominately in one of the five stages of development, while also identifying gaps in the earlier development of the national church.

For example, some of the fields in Africa would place themselves at Stage 4, the *Leaders* stage. However, they are struggling to make progress in this stage of development because of the lack of tithing in the local churches. The use of this diagnostic tool could help identify why tithing is not strongly taught. Perhaps discipleship in local churches has never been carried out successfully, or perhaps the use of small groups has not been encouraged. For many, especially in the heritage of John Wesley, attendance at a small mid-week group is closely associated with discipleship, membership and tithing.

One outcome of this evaluation, even when completed by missionary personnel alone, is that a field does not usually fit into any one stage alone. It becomes clear that, while evangelism and church planting are occurring in one place, postgraduate theological education might be occurring in another place on the same field. However, this should not hinder the assessment that the field has reached Stage 3, since a program for theological education has been achieved in the field's ministry.

The initial purpose for the development of *The 5 Stages of Missions* model was to assess when missionaries could exit from the field. However, as the stages were discussed we recognized that the missionaries do not necessarily have to leave the field; the goal is for them to move out of their positions of leadership. If missionaries are capable of moving from positions of leadership to positions of submission to national leadership, then they could continue to serve a constructive role on the field.

Unfortunately, in contrast to this goal of declining leadership, our experience compels us to admit that long-term missionaries usually gain influence over time. Regardless of the official position held by the long-term missionary, their words usually carry significant influence. This influence may be completely unintentional and unconscious, but the web of relationships and loyalties built over the previous years of ministry makes it difficult to avoid.

Couple this influence with the perception that international funding is secured through the missionaries, and it becomes clear why the ideal of a self-governing church is difficult to achieve while long-term missionaries remain. The presence of long-term missionaries generally works against the goal of indigenization.

In fact, it is not just the leadership role of the missionary that changes. The type of ministry and the need for longevity also changes. The gaps of language and culture are reduced as the national church workers become familiar with the missionaries' language and culture. For example, in the later Stages, theological professors can arrive on the mission field on Sunday and start teaching class on Monday because they are not required to go out into the villages to teach in the tribal language. The result is that the ideal type of missionary changes. The following *5 Stages and missionary leadership* chart attempts to capture these various issues.

The 5 Stages and missionary leadership (App. B)

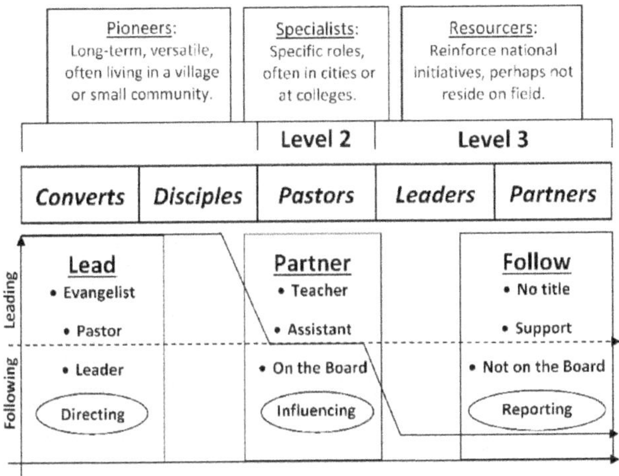

Once the status of the mission field is assessed, some form of objective grid could be put in place to make it clear to both missionaries and national leadership what expectation is held for missionaries. A preliminary grid was presented to the Global Partners' leadership team.

The 5 Stages accountability and leadership grid

	Stage 1 & 2 Directing	*Stage 3* Influencing	*Stage 4 & 5* Reporting
Field Leadership	Mission Council leads	National Board leads, Mission advises	National Board; no ex-officio missionaries
Mission Leadership	Mission Director leads	Mission Director leads	International Mission & field Team Leader
Missionary Assignment	Assigned by Mission Council	Negotiated between Mission and Church	Requested by National Board
Missionary Reporting	Report to Mission Council	To Mission and to National Board	Report to National Board
Finances	All funds through Mission banking	Separate Mission and church banking	Separate Mission and church banking
Fund Raising	Missionaries raise all funds	Missionaries & Nationals raise funds	Nationals raise funds

Some clear trends were emerging in discussions with the Leadership Council and with field missionaries. These understandings must be noted, because they influenced the further development of *The 5 Stages of Missions* model.

- *Exit* does not mean that there are no missionaries present. *Exit* means ceasing to fill previous roles, and usually means fewer missionaries present.

- To cease filling a previous role does not mean failure. Done properly, it equals "Success!" – A job well done!

- The presence of highly qualified missionaries can become a genuine disincentive to the development of the mission field. While the gifted missionary remains, national staff is unlikely to step forward.

- The influence exerted by a long-term or founding missionary on national church decision making is powerful, and not easily assessed by the missionaries themselves. Furthermore, they become a part of the system and cannot objectively evaluate their own influence. Therefore, the timing and success of the exit should be based on objective standards, perhaps even by an external body.

Review by national church leadership

In July 2002, the leadership of the Wesleyan Church in Southern Africa was gathered for a summit in Manzini, Swaziland. The majority of delegates were national church leaders from South Africa, Swaziland, Mozambique, Zambia and the Democratic Republic of Congo, accompanied by some mission leaders. *The 5 Stages of Missions* model was discussed at this forum. The model was quite enthusiastically received, especially by the national leaders and an animated discussion followed. However, the subdued participation of those missionaries present suggested that some felt under attack. Some notes were taken to capture the main points of the discussion.

- Leadership training should be incorporated into Stage 2.
- The national church needs infrastructure and a funding base if it is to assume missionary duties.
- The mission must multiply resources, not just knowledge.
- Sometimes it is the national church that resists the transition to Stage 4, not the missionaries.
- The missionary should have a purpose when he or she comes.
- Africans are inclined to first ask, "What resources are provided?"
- Financial support is expected to come from the missionary, and that is wrong.
- "The missionary never has the experience of doing his work under national church funding."
- There are three bodies involved in this progression: the national church, the missionaries, and the sending mission board. The sending board should have a strategy for sustainability.
- Stage 4 should be characterized by interdependence.
- Both the national church and the missionaries must understand the issue of empowerment.

- One of the missionaries quietly commented that perhaps the missionaries should just all go home.

In the 12 months after this summit *The 5 Stages of Missions* diagnostic work-sheet was used with three of the national boards represented at the Manzini Summit: Mozambique, Southern Africa and Zambia. Most felt that their field was at Stage 3 or 4, depending upon which province they were describing. None of the boards rated their field at Stage 5. The accumulated result of these powerful interactions was that some changes were made to the model and to the underlying thinking. These changes included the priority for economic empowerment, the acknowledgement that it is often the national church that resists indigenization, and the thought that all entities involved in the process must understand the need for indigenization.

The need for economic empowerment

The sentiment most often and most powerfully offered at the Manzini Summit was that missionaries do hand over responsibilities to national workers, but they typically make no provision for resources necessary for the responsibility. Situations were described where the missionary handed over a house but took all the furniture away, or where a national worker was given a significant role in discipleship but had no funding or equipment for travel, copying or typing. This sentiment was captured by the outburst, "The missionary never has the experience of doing his work under national church funding."

Since this meeting I have become more sensitive to the issue, especially when it applies to the institutions that the mission has established. Generally, tithing is perceived as the biblical base, and therefore the proper base, for church support. The biblical truth of tithing is not disputed here, but the question is asked, "What funding base is provided for schools, bible colleges and hospitals which are not supported through tithing?" The practice that continues to this day is for mission fields to be invited to raise funds in North America for these institutions, and until recently, the national church was encouraged to leave the fund-raising in the hands of the missionaries. This has produced a double dilemma, in that the national church is always dependent upon the parent country, and great power is placed in the hands of the missionaries. In recent years the North American economy suffered recession, and as a consequence, many institutions on the mission field suffered severe reductions in their subsidies, mostly with little or no warning. The result was that colleges struggled even to provide food for the staff and students. This crisis rendered long-term responsible planning for institutional development meaningless. Economic empowerment is a need strongly felt by the national church leadership, while it is a need that has been effectively overlooked by many mission agencies.

The national church resists indigenization

It was an interesting insight, articulated by one of the African leaders at the Manzini Summit, that it is often the African church that resists indigenization. This resistance is credited to several factors: loyalty to the missionaries, concern for fund-raising and unwillingness to accept responsibility.

There are real bonds of love and loyalty between the missionaries and the members of the national church. Any suggestion that the missionary should leave, or that the missionary should not receive due honor for his or her years of faithful service is too painful to embrace. Each generation agrees with indigenization in principle, but they sense that it will be appropriate at a later time.

For some there is the awareness that the missionary is their best international fund-raiser. When indigenization involves a declining number of missionaries, then there is a real financial cost to self-governance. Some would rather work with an ongoing missionary presence than work without the financial resources.

The reason most clearly articulated at the Manzini Summit for resisting indigenization, though, was the issue of responsibility. It can simply be easier to allow the missionaries to stay in control, because with that control comes responsibility. When there is a need, it is the mission's problem. Surely this mind-set is true of human nature, but it is difficult to imagine a condition more inconsistent with true discipleship.

The purpose for devoting this space to the insight that the national church often resists indigenization is because it is too easy to assume that the missionaries are the ones resisting indigenization. While at times it may be the missionaries, it is helpful to be reminded that the resistance comes from both sides. Bring this human reluctance together with the lack of economic empowerment, and it becomes clear why a mission work can spend half a century without making any real progress toward indigenization.

All involved must understand indigenization

The third insight to be highlighted is that there are three entities involved in the process of indigenization. These three are the national church, the missionaries and the sending agency. Some space has been devoted to the need for missionaries and national workers to adopt a priority of indigenization, but it is important to remember that the sending agency must be aware of, and committed to, this same goal.

The sending agency may be taken to include the sending congregations that finance overseas' missions as well as the agency that acts on their behalf to coordinate this task. The sending agency must understand the need for indigenization for several reasons: to celebrate a completed task, to support economic empowerment projects, to send educated work-teams and to release control.

If missionaries are to depart a field once their task is complete, it will be important that the sending church celebrates a "job well done" with the returning missionary, instead of questioning why they could not have stayed until retirement. This calls for a lot of education in the sending churches—both in the theory of indigenization and in an accurate knowledge of the condition of each mission field.

If sending congregations are to engage enthusiastically and meaningfully in mission field funding, they need to understand how projects that enable economic empowerment are essential to the larger goal of establishing a self-governing national church. We will return to this topic at a later time.

Short-term missionaries and work-teams must also understand the goals of the mission work. This particularly becomes an issue as the field reaches the later stages of maturity. Visiting work-teams regularly neglect consulting with national church leadership when making plans for ministry on the mission field, and when this happens, the work-team can do much damage to empowerment. It is possible for a well-intentioned work-team to achieve an impressive local project while creating dependency in the local church and showing public disdain for the national church leadership. One of the first lessons of cross-cultural ministry is to show appropriate honor to community leaders. Unfortunately, work-teams, in their desire to get down to the "grass-roots", too easily miss this fundamental rule. Work-teams which come from larger sending churches are especially prone to the mind-set that they are free from denominational structures, and if they bring the same mind-set to the mission field, they avoid field structures as well, at the cost of lasting effectiveness.

Finally, it takes a lot of understanding for the giving church to release projects into the hands of the national church after years of sponsorship. Furthermore, it takes a lot of effort for the missionary to explain to the sending church why the missionaries have not intervened to revive a cherished ministry or institution which is now waning under national church administration. Sometimes the higher ideal of national church maturity overrules the need to intervene. If the mission resumes control of the financial records, or of the school, or of the hospital when a problem arises, it can set the process of indigenization back by decades.

Including the sending church in the issues of mission field development can be time consuming. It often involves mission principles in which the sending church has no training, and sometimes the details of a dispute or failure cannot be fully disclosed to the overseas congregation. Consequently, faithful donors in the sending church are often motivated and led by the heart rather than by good mission strategy. When donors have loved and prayed for a ministry for years, it can be extremely difficult to explain to them why an institution had to be closed. It can be equally difficult to explain how a missionary can claim to have finished his or her task when there are still unsaved people left to reach. The answer lies in the missiological truth that the missionary's higher goal was to prepare a national church that is capable and willing to carry on the work of evangelism. Unfortunately, this answer does not easily satisfy donors who are led by a heart-felt compassion for the lost and who desire more immediate results.

When the higher goal is true indigenization, then there is also the growing question of sovereignty. The national church must have authority over its own ministry. For both the missionary and the sending agency, it is very easy to discuss submission to national church leadership as an objective goal. However, real submission is only truly revealed when the national church makes a decision to which the missionary or sending agency is fundamentally opposed. The outcome is that some agencies and missionaries that claim to ascribe to the principal of indigenization, in reality only place leadership in the national church's hands as long as the mission can reserve the power of veto. The power of veto, hidden behind a mask of indigenization, destroys the national church's motivation and ownership of the work.

In response to a growing awareness of these issues, *The 5 Stages of Missions* model included two note-worthy additions: the inclusion of *Emerging leaders* in Stage 3, and the inclusion of *Economic empowerment* in Stage 4.

Clarification of the goal

The author whose writing most closely mirrored this study was Dr. Tom Steffen. Steffen described stages in a similar way to *The 5 Stages of Missions* as he argued for the missionary's responsibility to phase out of the mission field. However, there was a fundamental difference in the goal described by Steffen and *The 5 Stages of Missions. The 5 Stages of Missions* comes to focus upon the goal of internationalization, not the withdrawal of the missionaries. In fact, the goal of indigenization as described by Henry Venn and Rufus Anderson likewise concludes with national administration of the field rather than international engagement in the Great Commission.

The goal of *The 5 Stages of Missions* has come to be defined as developing the mission field until it stands as a full partner in the work of international missions. The work of missions is complete when the leader of the mission field and the leader of the original sending church can relate to each other as genuine peers. This does not mean that Steffen does not have these same priorities, but rather that the process of refining *The 5 Stages of Missions* has made us more conscious that phasing out is not enough. Withdrawal from the field and shifting missionary resources onto a new field alone will result in a slow process of addition as the parent church gradually reaches into new countries. On the other hand, empowering full partners in international missionary endeavors is likened to the process of multiplication with an increasing outreach to the world.

As a result of this refining, the phrase *International leadership* has been added to Stage 5. Sharing in the international task of global evangelism is the final symptom of maturity. It would be difficult to be an international leader without an international missionary outreach.

Modern Missions

The effectiveness of past generations of Christian missions means that today we are increasingly being approached by groups of national believers around the globe who want to join the wider body and come under the perceived benefits of an international structure. This is especially true in Africa and required us to revise our application of *The 5 Stages of Missions*. At the same time, with the passing of the colonial era and the refocus toward the 10/40 window, missionaries are increasingly going to countries where Islam and Hinduism control the political climate, and where overt evangelism is not tolerated. Other countries are hardened to the Gospel because of communism, secularism or lifeless Christianity. How then does the *5 Stages* model serve us in this shifting climate of missions?

The answer is found by thinking of the stages as components in missions rather than as stages; components that can be reordered but still serve the purpose of outlining the essentials of a healthy ministry? Some hypothetical situations will illustrate this concept:

1. Missionaries may enter a field at the invitation of an existing group of believers to assist them in transition to, and alignment with, an international network or denomination.

2. Missionaries may seek to start a new ministry in a country that has a substantial Christian history and a high level of education, but a failing evangelical fervor.

3. Missionaries may seek to start a new ministry in a culture that is outwardly antagonistic to Christianity and conversion. In this setting, they feel that the church must remain underground.

Integrating an existing group

In the first scenario, the mission is welcoming an existing group of believers into the international body. Perhaps the new group already has a number of churches, and even has its own bible college in place. The conclusion then might be that they are already at Stage 3 in their development. The work that remains may be only to assist in higher education in ministry related areas and with some form of economic empowerment so that they can more adequately enter into international ministry.

Even in this case though, it would be common for the mission agency to enter with a sense of caution. The members of the various congregations may not properly understand saving faith or the pastoral team may not exhibit the depth of spirituality that should be expected of Christian leaders. In this case *The 5 Stages of Missions* can serve a diagnostic purpose for the existing work as well as a visionary purpose for future ministry.

The result would be that some remedial work needs to be done in Stages 1 and 2, before Stage 3 can be properly completed and the transition to higher stages effected. The missionary may need to undertake some diplomatic, but extensive evangelism and discipleship before a pool of spiritually-minded leaders is ready to move ahead internationally.

Using the 5 Stages when entering at Stage 3

In fact, any national church or mission agency may find it useful to review their progress using the *5 Stages* as a diagnostic tool. The early missionaries may have been excellent evangelists but failed to adequately train their converts to be evangelists. The result might be that the missionaries have moved onto discipleship and pastoral training while no one has seriously taken up the task of evangelism. Or perhaps, after many decades it may be realized that tithing is still not practiced by the local congregations. This might be hindering the church from moving into Stage 4, but in reality, it can be traced back to the failure to teach consecration or a failure to establish any form of small group ministry in the local churches. It would be advisable to attempt an objective diagnosis first, rather than making an assessment based on surface appearances or optimistic reports. Furthermore, if a field shows signs of being spread across several or all stages, then a simple assignment may not be immediately possible.

Using the 5 Stages when entering at stage 3

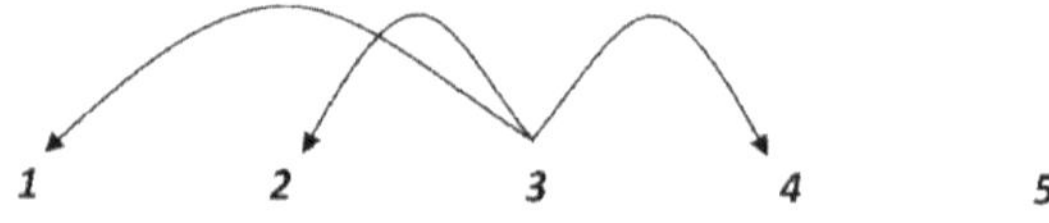

Converts	Disciples	Pastors	Leaders	Partners
First contacts:	***Teach believers:***	***Prepare pastors:***	***Replace & redeploy:***	***International ministry:***
• Relationships • Evangelism • Ministries of compassion • Church planting	• Teaching & preaching • Consecration • Small groups • Literature	• TEE • Bible schools • Ordination • Emerging leaders	• Nationals to post-grad level • Re-assign expatriates • Economic empowerment	• Missions to other cultures • Missions to other nations • International leaders

To use the *5 Stages* as a diagnostic tool, have the church or mission leadership complete the following worksheet.

5 Stages diagnostic worksheet (App. C)

5 Stages of Missions

Diagnostic Worksheet

Date: ___________

Leadership team or Board: ______________________________

3 - Task fully completed and functioning well
2 - Task has been started and only needs minor attention
1 - Task has been started, but needs substantial rework
0 - Very little progress made with task

CONVERTS		***DISCIPLES***		***PASTORS***		***LEADERS***		***PARTNERS***	
First contacts:		***Teach believers:***		***Prepare pastors:***		***Replace & redeploy:***		***International ministry:***	
	3-0		3-0		3-0		3-0		3-0
Relationships		Teaching & preaching		TEE		Nationals to post-grad level		Missions to other cultures	
Evangelism		Consecration		Bible schools		Re-assign expatriates		Missions to other nations	
Ministries of compassion		Small groups		Ordination		Economic empowerment		International leaders	
Church planting		Literature		Emerging leaders					

As a general principal, include as many of the leadership team as possible. The more ownership of the process there is, the more likely the church is to address issues that are identified.

The board members should rate each element of the stages on a scale of 1 to 3. Collate the responses and print the result out on a single sheet. The result from a survey of ten church leaders may look something like the following sample form, with major deficiencies revealed.

Sample diagnostic worksheet

CONVERTS		***DISCIPLES***		***PASTORS***		***LEADERS***		***PARTNERS***	
First contacts:		***Teach believers:***		***Prepare pastors:***		***Replace & redeploy:***		***International ministry:***	
	30		30		30		30		30
Relationships	19	Teaching & preaching	23	TEE	0	Nationals to post-grad level	10	Missions to other cultures	26
Evangelism	22	Consecration	16	Bible schools	28	Re-assign expatriates	7	Missions to other nations	3
Ministries of compassion	11	Small groups	3	Ordination	29	Economic empowerment	0	International leaders	7
Church planting	18	Literature	5	Emerging leaders	23				

From this, the board has identified several key elements that require attention:

- Insufficient attention has been given to ministries of compassion and development. Apart from the Christian obligation to care for those who are suffering, church leaders should be aware that community development has a great deal of impact on local church economic empowerment.

- Establishment of small groups has never been adequately attempted in this setting. Small group involvement enhances the congregation's ownership of the local church, and directly impacts attendance, ministry and tithing.

- Discipleship is hindered by the lack of good literature. The answer may simply be to source the bulk of the materials from other publishers. However, locally produced, purpose-designed literature may be necessary when focusing on the group's distinctive.

- No program for training pastors through in-service has been developed.

- Stages 4 and 5 are where the church needs to intentionally develop for the future.

An action plan should then be produced that would address deficiencies in the current ministry and to prepare for the next stage of development. For example:

- The National Church Board will employ a Christian Education Director whose primary tasks will be the promotion of an Adult Sunday School ministry and the sourcing of suitable literature.

- The mission will initiate negotiations with an NGO (non-government organization) to provide micro-enterprise loans in rural villages where the church has a stable leadership team.

- The Bible College is commissioned to prepare a proposal for the delivery of ordination courses by extension in five centers around the country.

- The National Church Board shall recommend five candidates and seek international scholarships for advanced theological training, in preparation for the shift into Stage 4 in the coming years.

New ministry in a formerly Christian country

In the second scenario missionaries are entering a country where there is a long Christian heritage, but which evidences powerless church life today. In this country, which has benefited from advanced civilization for many centuries, there is a generally high level of education and health care. Ministries of compassion may not be as necessary, though community development may still prove to be the key to access to the country and credibility in the community.

A superficial assessment might conclude that *The 5 Stages of Missions* are irrelevant since the population already has international access and confidence. On further reflection though, we see that the *5 Stages* serves as a useful tool for evaluation of the ministry that is in place. At least initially, the evaluation might lead to a focus on remedial work rather than future vision.

Using the 5 Stages when entering at Stage 4

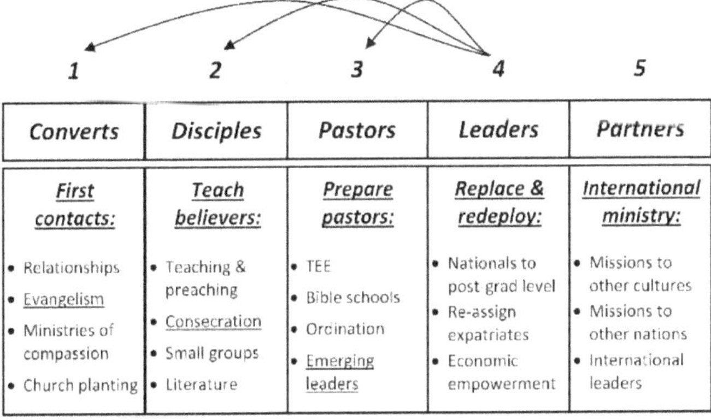

1	2	3	4	5
Converts	*Disciples*	*Pastors*	*Leaders*	*Partners*
First contacts:	*Teach believers:*	*Prepare pastors:*	*Replace & redeploy:*	*International ministry:*
• Relationships • Evangelism • Ministries of compassion • Church planting	• Teaching & preaching • Consecration • Small groups • Literature	• TEE • Bible schools • Ordination • Emerging leaders	• Nationals to post grad level • Re-assign expatriates • Economic empowerment	• Missions to other cultures • Missions to other nations • International leaders

With further study though, it can be seen that education alone is not the goal of Stage 4. Secular education is not the same as theological education, and theological education does not necessarily equate with Christian experience and commitment. Perhaps the church is more correctly at Stage 2, in need of discipling, despite the presence of an educated leadership. The mission may well need to guide the church systematically through basic issues of conversion and discipleship. In that case, *The 5 Stages of Missions* would be quite essential in identifying the deficiencies and plotting an action plan for intervention.

Missions in persecution

The modern focus of Christian missions toward Islamic countries is being undertaken with admirable ingenuity. The use of "creative access" enables Christians to quietly enter countries where Christian missionaries are not welcome. The Church quietly grows as home groups and cell-churches. People who have known oppression are coming to know the Living God. It is to be celebrated.

However, if the implication is drawn that the development of international leaders and missions is not relevant to the underground church, then this is unhealthy Christianity. Let us be careful and respectful of those in life-threatening situations but let us not delude ourselves that there is some peculiar risk in our generation. The strategy of quiet entry will not satisfy the demands of the Gospel for long, regardless of the risk. The Church may need to be planted underground, but by nature it must reach upward and outward. The Gospel will not hide under a bushel for long.

We are not promoting reckless endangerment of missionaries or national Christians in persecuted countries. However, we do desire to remind the mission community that God is bigger than oppressive governments. God raised up an Abraham Lincoln, a Nelson Mandela and a Mikhail Gorbachev, each in their generation, and God will do so again. Imagine what would happen if, in response to the current rise of terrorism, the Islamic community chose to renounce violence. Imagine if the door swung open in Islamic countries as quickly as it did in communist USSR! What a time for the church to be on site, with a vision and strategy for international outreach.

The persecuted Church should never allow itself to think that it can rest at the end of the Gospel food-chain. No mission field should remain merely as receivers of the Gospel. Maturity is to become fully engaged in the Great Commission. Every field has the obligation to become senders of missionaries. It might take a century of quiet preparation, but in the end the Gospel will overcome... or be overcome. If it does take a century, there is even more need for a *5 Stages* type of vision to hold before the missionaries and national believers alike.

The 5 components of missions

The 5 Stages of Missions has been developed in the light of two centuries of evangelical missionary theory and experience. However, strategies of foreign missions are continually changing. One practical example of this might be seen in the fact that missionaries to Africa in the past centuries have generally gone to tribal peoples who have a strong traditional awareness of the supernatural. The challenge therefore, was not to convince them of a god, but to lead them to the true God. Sometimes this was achieved through a display of power (colonial or supernatural), and sometimes it was accomplished through years of presence and modeling. However, many missions today go to people who are agnostic or atheistic, especially in the wake of materialism and communism. The challenge in these situations is to first awaken a hunger for the supernatural before conversion can take place. This awakening is usually achieved in the context of relationships, as believers model a fulfilled life. When serving in these modern cultures, missionaries question the validity of traditional missionary models, especially since, in their setting, the work begins with relationship and discipleship, rather than conversion.

This should not be the source of contention though, because in reality, relationship and discipleship precede conversion to some degree in every missionary outreach. Rather, let us think of the *5 Stages* as *5 Components* of missions. The term *Stages* implies some chronological progression, while the term *components* allows more flexibility. Suppose then, that the Great Commission of Matthew 28: 19–20 is taken as the goal of missions. To make disciples of other nations sums up the goal of missions. In that case we might say that making disciples is the total goal, as the following chart illustrates.

The goal of missions (App. D)

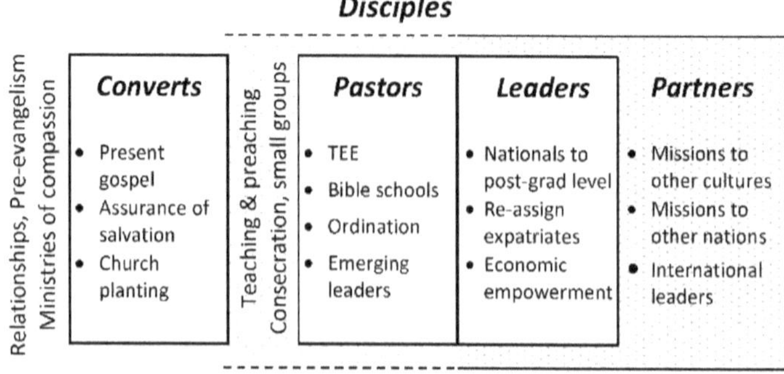

Section III: IMPLICATIONS OF THE MODEL

Chapter 4: **How long?**

The question that seems to be asked most often is how long indigenization should take. Is it possible to plant an indigenous church in one year and then move on? Should a mission agency plan a 15-year presence on a field? If the mission is still present after 100 years, has it failed to indigenize?

This topic has drawn a number of opinions over the past century. None seems to have been more widely quoted than Rolland Allen's thesis that we should be able to do as the Apostle Paul did; enter a city, plant a church, and depart in around 3 months. He makes the statement that "Our difficulty is that we have not yet tried St. Paul's method anywhere" (Allen, 1998: 25). This is such a foundational issue and an extreme claim that time must be given to examine the issue of "How long?" If Allen is correct, then it should revolutionize mission practice. If he is not correct, then it is time to lay this claim to rest.

The Apostle Paul's mission strategy

It is instructive to chart the record of Paul's ministry found in the book of Acts. The following chart does not include every province, island, or city to which Paul's journeys took him as this would have added unnecessary detail. Instead the review is limited to the places where church planting activity was recorded. Some noteworthy glimpses into Paul's missionary strategy emerge in this simple exercise.

The Apostle Paul's Missionary Journeys

First Journey	***Initial Contact***	***Focus Group***	***Depart***	***Elders***	***Return Visit***
13:4–5 Salamis	Synagogues	No church named			No return
13:6–12 Paphos	Political interview				No return
13:13 Perga			Left John		
13:14–52 P. Antioch	Synagogue	Gentiles & Jews	Expelled	Second visit	14:21, 22 16:4, 19:1
14:1–5 Iconium	Synagogue	Gentiles & Jews	Fled	Second visit	14:21, 22 16:2, 19:1
14:6–20 Lystra	Public healing	Disturbance	Stoned	Second visit	14:21, 22 16:1, 19:1
14:21 Derbe	Preached (synagogue?)	Many disciples	Travel on		16:1 19:1
14:25 Perga	Preached (synagogue?)				14:21, 22

Second Journey	***Initial Contact***	***Focus Group***	***Depart***	***Elders***	***Return Visit***
16:7–10 Troas		No church named			20:2, 6
16:13–40 Philippi	Place of Prayer	Group of believers	Flogged		20:2–3
17:1–10 Thess.	Synagogue	Gentiles & Jews	After riot		20:2–3
17:10–14 Berea	Synagogue	Gentiles & Jews	Fled mob		20:2–3
17:15–34 Athens	Synagogue & publicly	Few believers	Few fruit		20:2–3
18:1–18 Corinth	Synagogue	Gentiles & Jews	1 1/2 yrs	Apollos sent	20:2–3
18:19–21 Ephesus	Synagogue		Returned 3rd trip	Priscilla Aquila	19:1–20:2 20:17–38
18:22 Caesarea		Existing church			

The Apostle Paul's Missionary Journeys cont...

Third Journey	***Initial Contact***	***Focus Group***	***Depart***	***Elders***	***Return Visit***
19:1–20:1 Ephesus	Believers & Synagogue	Gentiles & Jews	After riot	Stayed 2 years	20:17–38
21:3–6 Tyre		Existing church			
21:7 Ptolemais		Existing church			
21:8–14 Caesarea		Existing church			

To Rome	***Initial Contact***	***Focus Group***	***Depart***	***Elders***	***Return Visit***
27–28:10 Malta	Miracles		A prisoner	Stayed 3 months	
28:13–14 Puteoli		Existing church	A prisoner		
28:14–31 Rome	Gathered the Jews	Gentiles & Jews		Stayed 2 years	

Start in the Synagogues

From the outset of these journeys, Paul and Barnabas go to the synagogues as their first point of contact in a new community. By the time they reach the province of Pisidia the strategy is established, "At Iconium Paul and Barnabas went as usual into the Jewish synagogue" (Acts 14: 5). In the second journey, now separated from Barnabas, Paul continues this strategy.

When they had passed through Amphipolis and Apollonia, they came to Thessalonica, where there was a Jewish synagogue. As his custom was, Paul went into the synagogue, and on three Sabbath days he reasoned with them from the Scriptures, explaining and proving that the Christ had to suffer and rise from the dead (Acts 17: 2).

In Lystra, Derbe and Perga the text does not specify that they went to the synagogue, although the practice has been established prior to that time. In the absence of any other invitation to preach, we can assume that they followed the practice already established.

In fact, it can be seen in the chart that the response to the Gospel was noticeably limited when Paul did not initiate his visit by preaching in the synagogue (or the place of prayer). In Paphos a political interview turned into a supernatural struggle with Elymas; in Lystra great disturbance occurred after a public healing; and in Athens only "a few men became followers" after his eloquent speech at the Areopagus.

Paul's initial contact at the synagogue reveals a related part of Paul's strategy. "Paul gave his chief attention to the cities" (LaTourette, 1999: 73).

> St. Paul's theory of evangelizing a province was not to preach in every place in it himself, but to establish centres of Christian life in two or three important places from which the knowledge might spread into the country around (Allen, 1998: 12).

Go beyond the Synagogue

The biblical record shows that Paul quickly adopted a strategy of reaching beyond the synagogue. There is no record in the book of Acts of any churches planted in Cyprus, the first province visited on the first journey, despite Paul and Barnabas preaching in a number of synagogues throughout the island. Furthermore, there is no record of Paul ever returning to Cyprus after this one visit. It was Barnabas who returned there in Acts 15: 39, accompanied by John Mark, after a sharp disagreement with Paul.

It seems clear that their experience in Cyprus was not fulfilling, which resulted in a significant adaptation to the strategy. This is highlighted by two changes; John Mark left the team and Paul started to plant churches independent of the synagogue immediately after Cyprus. This suggests that the transition from Cyprus to Pisidia marks a significant new phase in Paul's strategy.

> The most natural explanation of the return of John Mark from Perga is that he turned back because he saw that after the crisis at Paphos St. Paul was become the real leader of the mission in the place of his own cousin, Barnabas, and was prepared both to preach outside the synagogue to Gentiles with greater freedom than he had anticipated, and to admit Gentiles into fellowship on terms which he was hardly proposing to accept (Allen, 1998: 10).

The strategy, which had started with the visit to the synagogue, was now expanded and no longer expected to stay in the synagogue. Those who would accept Christ from within the synagogue would become the nucleus of the Church, meeting separately from the synagogue.

When it is time to leave

It is difficult, based upon the biblical evidence, to claim that Paul had any particular strategy for departure from a church plant. In most cases he stayed until there was a real attack upon himself or the congregation. The evidence suggests that Paul's strategy, at least in his early journeys, was simply to stay until he was driven out. It may be that he developed an expectation in later journeys that his stay would be short, but the text does not support the idea that he worked to a predetermined exit strategy.

The three exceptions to this "stay until driven out" practice are in Derbe, Perga, and Athens, and there are viable alternative reasons for his departure from those cities. The departure from Perga after preaching there seems to have simply been that Paul's group was already committed to travel plans to return to their sending church. However, the other two exceptions reveal some interesting strategic insights.

In Derbe, Paul seems to have realized that he had left churches in Pisidian Antioch, Iconium and Lystra without leadership. It is likely that it was in Derbe that Paul first adopted a conscious strategy of appointing local leadership in churches when he left. From Derbe he turned back to appoint elders in the previous three centers. This marks the start of a significant part of Paul's missionary strategy. It must have been very tempting for Paul to simply travel east from Derbe, through his home province of Cilicia, to the sending church in Antioch. However, Paul and Barnabas chose the long route west in response to the urgent need for local church leadership in the cities they had already visited.

Paul's departure from Athens is similarly instructive. Paul seems to have been quite disappointed by his ministry at the Areopagus; perhaps even reprimanded by the Lord. Paul left Athens quickly and went on to preach in Corinth. Paul's message was simplified after Athens, as he states at a later time when he writes to the Corinthian Church:

> When I came to you, brothers, I did not come with eloquence or superior wisdom as I proclaimed to you

> the testimony about God. For I resolved to know nothing while I was with you except Jesus Christ and him crucified. I came to you in weakness and fear, and with much trembling. My message and my preaching were not with wise and persuasive words, but with a demonstration of the Spirit's power, so that your faith might not rest on men's wisdom, but on God's power (1 Corinthians 2: 1–5).

Paul's ministry in Corinth provides a significant glimpse into Paul's exit strategy itself because it is the first church where Paul settles down for an extended time. Clearly, he has grown accustomed to departing rapidly, driven by persecution, to the extent that the Lord had to give Paul a special vision to convince him to settle.

> One night the Lord spoke to Paul in a vision: "Do not be afraid; keep on speaking, do not be silent. For I am with you, and no one is going to attack and harm you, because I have many people in this city." So Paul stayed for a year and a half, teaching them the word of God (Acts 18: 9–11).

Sometime later, the Jews did attack Paul though, and this is followed by Paul's departure from Corinth. The evidence suggests that Paul allowed God to direct the timing of his departure, and usually through persecution. He stayed as long as it was safe to do so. When the severity of Paul's beatings in other cities is considered, it is not a surprise that he adopted this strategy. When persecution arose, Paul was in real mortal danger. Comprehending just how real the danger was adds weight to Paul's words above, "I came to you in weakness and fear, and with much trembling."

Appointing Elders

Paul's practice of appointing elders to lead the church, while he himself moved on to a new church planting opportunity, is well recognized. However, our chart gives us some insight into this as well.

As has been stated earlier, it is clear that on his first journey, Paul left Pisidian Antioch, Iconium and Lystra without appointing local leadership. It is in Derbe that he realized this need and returned for this purpose. This suggests that this part of Paul's strategy was not carefully planned. Indeed, if Paul's departure was a reaction to persecution, rather than a strategic decision, then the need for elders was also a necessity that arose in the course of the work. Paul was engaged in on-field strategic refinement.

There is no other reference to the appointment of elders in the book of Acts, but we do find reference to the practice in the Epistles. Paul writes to Titus, "The reason I left you in Crete was to straighten out what was left unfinished and appoint elders in every town, as I directed you" (Titus 1: 5). Once again, Paul had already left the church plant and in retrospect, is making arrangement for the appointment of elders. The appointment of elders was a necessary development in Paul's missiology, as a result of rapid departures brought on by persecution. It was not an integral part of some pre-planned strategy. Paul was adapting as he went along.

A related adaptation in Paul's missiology is the growing group of disciples that accompany him. On the second journey he starts out with Titus, and recruits Timothy in Lystra (Acts 15: 40–16: 1). By the time Paul is ready to leave Greece on his third journey, "He was accompanied by Sopater son of Pyrrhus from Berea, Aristarchus and Secundus from Thessalonica, Gaius from Derbe, Timothy also, and Tychicus and Trophimus from the province of Asia" (Acts 20: 4). We also understand that Luke was with Paul as his scribe, and Titus was likely off on commission to one of the new churches. This growing number of disciples reveals a second part of Paul's strategy to provide leadership in young churches. These become Paul's representatives. He had a growing web of supervision for the new churches (Acts 17: 4, 1 Corinthians 4: 17, 1 Timothy 1: 3). The third part of Paul's supervision was to write to the new churches—a strategy that resulted in a substantial portion of the New Testament.

Multiplying churches

As Paul's ministry continued it became clear that others were taking on the challenge of church planting too. There is a hint of this in his visits to Troas.

When Paul first traveled through Troas he did not have time to attend the synagogue or start a church, because upon arrival in Troas a vision of a man in Macedonia created such urgency that they stayed just one night (Acts 16: 7–10). However, on Paul's second visit to Troas, on his return from Greece, he found a well-established church and stayed for a week. It was at the Troas all-night preaching session that Paul raised Eutychus from the dead after the young man fell asleep and out of a window (Acts 20: 6–12). The evidence does not suggest that Paul planted the church in Troas.

The cities of Caesarea, Tyre and Ptolemais also have existing churches. This is not a surprise though, since we already know of the work on the Syrian coast by Phillip the Evangelist and the Apostle Peter. However, it is interesting to see that Paul found an existing church in Puteoli, near Rome, when he arrived as a prisoner in that city. Clearly someone had gone ahead of Paul to initiate the work in Italy, leap-frogging Paul's missionary journeys in Asia, Macedonia and Greece.

The return visits

It is well documented that Paul made a priority of return visits to church plants. In fact, most of Paul's writings in the New Testament are a result of his continuing contact with the churches. As we have already established, when he couldn't visit personally, Paul wrote or sent one of his team with authority to govern the church. This might seem like a natural strategy but consider how local church leaders today might react to return visits from the founding pastor. This was fairly extreme supervision if we are to accept that these churches were self-governing at this stage. It should be noted however, that repeat visits were not permitted to become extended stays. Paul had other cities in which to preach.

One exception to this policy of brief return visits should be noted. Paul's initial visit to Ephesus resulted in his promise to return, which he did with some haste. In this case, the second visit should properly be considered the founding visit. It is extraordinary to note that, despite leaving Priscilla and Aquila there to teach, the church had still not heard about the Holy Spirit when Paul returned in chapter 19. "We have not even heard that there is a Holy Spirit" (Acts 19: 2). This raises a question about the depth of Priscilla and Aquila's own understanding of the Gospel and highlights the danger of premature departure.

The Apostle Paul's strategy

Paul
1. Enter synagogue
2. Form separate church
3. Appoint leaders after forced departure
4. Supervision and occasional visits

This summary of Paul's missionary journeys, though not exhaustive, has yielded helpful insights into the Apostle Paul's missionary strategy. Paul clearly went to synagogues, to those with whom he had cultural, linguistic and religious bridges, as his first point of contact. He then drew Jewish and Gentile believers into a separate church. Paul then stayed as long as his situation allowed, though he expected his visits to be only a matter of months. When forced to leave, Paul would appoint elders to local leadership and would maintain his own influence through brief personal visits, through the visit of one of his pastoral team and through letters.

The circumstances that dictated Paul's ministry continued for several centuries. However, "during the two or three centuries after the death of Paul, there is no evidence of any carefully defined mission method in use" (Mathews 1990: 297). Nonetheless, history speaks of rapid expansion of the church across the Roman Empire until about 500AD (LaTourette, 1999: 75, 76, 97).

This expansion across the Roman Empire occurred in a unique context that greatly impacted the mission strategy employed.

- Greek language was employed across the empire, which enabled the message to be conveyed without periods of language learning.
- Jewish synagogues had been spread across the empire in the Diaspora, which provided an immediate and "singular opportunity" for a ready audience (Allen, 1998: 15).
- The Old Testament had been translated into Greek in the Septuagint, so the urgency of Bible translation was greatly reduced. Paul, for example, never translated the Bible.
- As Christianity became more independent of its Jewish roots, the trade routes across the Empire provided access.
- Persecution was a dominant feature throughout the first three centuries of the period – first from the Jewish leaders, and later from the Roman government as Christianity grew and the connection to Judaism faded.

The bridges of language and culture, and sometimes even the Old Testament scriptures, should be acknowledged as significant elements in the mission strategy of the first millennium.

Rolland Allen on Paul's mission strategy

With this perspective on the missionary work of the Apostle Paul, we are ready to look closer at the claims that all missionaries should follow Paul's example. In doing this we can see that Rolland Allen has overstated some of the methods and conditions of Paul's ministry.

Jewish opposition is overstated

To show that Paul had no advantage in going to the Jewish synagogue, Allen argues that "the moment he delivered this message the whole Jewish community rose up against him, expelling him, and sought to take his life as a blasphemer of God" (Allen, 1998: 20). It is simply not true that the "whole Jewish community rose up against" Paul. It would be more accurate to say that Paul divided the Jewish community and could not continue to minister in the synagogue. Some went with Paul; many stayed in the synagogue, but some did go with Paul.

The value of Jewish converts is understated

To play down the benefit of the presence of the synagogue and the God-fearing Greeks, Allen argues that these things only blessed the new church with "a few people who could read the Old Testament..." (Allen, 1998: 22). This argument fails to acknowledge the role played by Jewish workers such as Barnabas, Silas, Apollos, Priscilla and Aquila, and even Timothy (whose mother was Jewish). It seems clear that Paul leaned heavily upon those trained in the Jewish tradition.

Paul's social advantages are understated

Even if the presence of the synagogue or God-fearing Greeks was not a significant advantage to Paul, as Allen argued, Allen's own words show that Paul had other extraordinary advantages. "He did not enter these great cities as a mere stranger. He came as a member of a family, as a member of a powerful and highly privileged association" (Allen, 1998: 15).

> Everywhere Roman government went hand in hand with Greek education. This education provided St. Paul with his medium of communication. There is no evidence of any attempt to translate the Scriptures into the provincial dialects of Asia Minor (Allen, 1998: 14).

Clearly Paul had huge advantages of social profile, common language, shared culture, literacy, political stability, and a ready-made audience.

> Allen never understood that Paul was riding the crest of the New Testament people movement to Christ, and under those circumstances indigenous church methods worked very well (McGavran in Branner, 1972: 165–66).

Paul's ability to exit quickly is overstated

In demonstrating how quickly Paul allowed a church to be self-governing, Allen describes Paul's ministry in Lystra, where, after the initial church plant, he visited for only short periods, sometimes with years between visits (Allen, 1998: 84). Yet, soon after Allen concedes "They sorely needed visits and instruction, and they received them. I have no doubt that he was in constant communication with them by one means or another" (Allen, 1998: 86). Clearly Paul was not able to simply move on after a few months.

Bridged and Unbridged Missions

It seems that Roland Allen did not differentiate between two distinct types of international mission work, which we shall title: *Bridged Missions* and *Unbridged Missions*. The spread of the Gospel throughout countries under common political dominion was the dominant method of church expansion for the first millennium of the Christian Church, so much so that this method of missions requires a specific classification: *Bridged Missions*. The use of cultural and political bridges greatly impacts exit from a mission field, because in the right setting, such as Paul's Roman world, rapid entry and rapid exit become possible.

However, when the Gospel is introduced where there are few or no social or political bridges, there is necessarily a difference in entry and exit strategies and in the time-frame needed for successful discipleship. The training of local leaders becomes a life's work, not simply a selection process. The often-lengthy process of preparing local workers becomes one of the key strategic differences between *Bridged Missions* and missions into new cultures. The term *Unbridged Missions* can be coined to describe the work of carrying the Gospel across barriers of politics, culture, language, literacy and economic disparity.

As mentioned earlier, Allen claims that the Apostle Paul's methods have not been tried in modern missions (Allen, 1998: 25). This claim does not stand up to inspection though, if it is understood that Paul was involved in *Bridged Missions*. The work that John Wesley did in leading a new church out of the Church of England is comparable to Paul's ministry. Wesley, with help from his team, drew upon his special advantage as a minister of the Anglican Church to establish a new church, not just in England, but in Ireland, Wales and in the United States of America. Because Wesley was working across solid bridges he was able to proceed very rapidly indeed. Clearly this sort of church growth would not have been possible if Wesley had first been required to learn a language, build a home, construct an alphabet, translate the Bible, develop literacy, and then train pastors. Neither would Paul's ministry have followed the same patterns if he had been required to build those foundations of typical *Unbridged Missions*.

In reflection upon this same issue, George Peters describes Paul's ministry as Home Missions, and concludes that, "The beautiful idea 'to do as Paul did it' may betray more naiveté than wisdom, more idealism than realism (Peters, 1972: 239).

Perhaps the error in the myth of Paul's missiology lies in one of Allen's early statements, "Either we must drag down St. Paul from his pedestal as the great missionary, or else we must acknowledge that there is in his work that quality of universality" (Allen, 1998: 5). Allen's error lies in placing Paul on a pedestal as *the great missionary*. Paul was, without question, *the great theologian*, but to overstate his missiological genius out of reverence does missions a disservice. Paul's great genius, and his unsurpassed gift to the church, was his ability to separate Grace from the Law; the eternal truths of the Gospel from cultural applications of those truths. The evidence suggests, though, that Paul was simply a pragmatic missiologist who adjusted his strategy as he traveled; always driven by passion and persecution.

The irony is that Roland Allen also salutes the truth of Paul's theological genius. Allen speaks at length about Paul's unwillingness to appeal to the Ten Commandments or to the rulings of the Jerusalem Council when dealing with new believers in Corinth. Instead Paul taught the power and relationship of the Spirit of God (Allen, 1998: 113–14).

This is powerful theology, and it is essential to effective missiology. The ability to go to the mission field and leave one's own cultural applications behind is quite rare. That the Spirit of God is better equipped to apply biblical truth to a new culture than any missionary is a lesson in which all missionary candidates should be saturated. If Allen could have arrived at this same conclusion without overstating Paul's method of church planting, the mission community might have been more open to receive this valuable lesson.

On this valuable message of trusting the Holy Spirit to provide better supervision for the Church than missionaries could do, Allen summarizes well:

> Nevertheless the fear haunts us that if we allowed our converts, though they might be illiterate men, to teach freely what they had learned, the doctrine might spread like wildfire, and the country might be covered with multitudes of groups of men calling themselves Christians, but really be ignorant of the first principles of Christ; and that thus the Church and her doctrine might be swamped, as it were, with a flood of ignorance (Allen, 1997: 52).

How long should it take to work through *The 5 Stages of Missions*? It depends upon the conditions that are encountered upon arrival. It depends upon the bridges that need to be crossed to reach the new culture. It depends upon the political and social development of the country. It depends upon the missionary vision for indigenization and the national believers' response to the claims of the Gospel. Significant factors include:

- The time required for language acquisition and translation work.

- The literacy level of the people. It is difficult to progress beyond Stages 2 or 3 without a functioning system of education in the country.

- The economic condition of the country. It is difficult to progress beyond dependency without a tithing base and a national funding strategy for ministerial training institutions, or a workable alternative to the use of institutions.

- The political outlook of the government. It is very difficult to progress far beyond Stage 2 if it is against the law to convert, to mix with people of other race, or to provide education for certain sections of society.

Having said these things, we are aware that the national church often grows rapidly during times of persecution and in the absence of missionaries. This is the work of the Spirit of God. The task then, is to accept the challenge of missions as a long-term commitment but seek to develop self-governance and self-funding as quickly as possible. Perhaps the Spirit will reward you with rapid church growth and community development, and you can exit sooner than expected.

The next chapter will include reference to one other factor that impacts this discussion about timing. If the mission stays beyond one generation of missionaries or local converts, new dynamics enter into the equation. Systems of missionary control become embedded; a generation grows up with no other model than submission to missionaries, and dependency or rebellion result.

Chapter 5: **Implications for mission agencies**

The 5 Stages of Missions highlights the fundamental shift in the relationship between the mission agency and the national church in the maturing process of a mission field. Through to Stage 3, authority and power are primarily in the hands of the missionaries. Although the missionaries progress through a range of ministries from evangelism to bible school teaching, they still carry primary authority over the field. However, as the field enters into Stage 4, power and responsibility transfers to the national church leaders. This transfer does not always happen easily, and even where there is a conscious commitment to the transfer, it can take some time.

Three significant issues in this shift of power deserve special attention: the role of missionaries, the eras of missions and, in the following chapter, the sharing of resources.

The role of missionaries

The first three stages of making converts, disciples and pastors appear to have been more readily applied on the mission field than the last two stages of making leaders and partners. That is not to suggest that the work of making converts, disciples or pastors was easy, just that the missionaries intuitively understood this component of their work. Even if it took fifty years to progress through issues of disease, poverty, translation, literacy or persecution, the missionaries could work away at it with a clear sense of purpose. However, the transition to Stage 4: making *Leaders* appears to have been the point of blockage in mission work because transitioning to national leadership did not come intuitively. In some cases, the transition was actively resisted.

When the early mission endeavor produced converts, it was a time of celebration. It was then not difficult to "work yourself out of a job" by becoming the pastor and commissioning the new disciples to become the soul-winners. Equally, as the work grew, and some disciples become ready for pastoral duties, it was not difficult to take another step back by becoming the bible college teacher. In the first three stages the missionaries remained ahead of the national church in both authority and in prestige, and it was likely that they were still controlling the overall direction of the field. It is in Stage 4 that the authority and prestige shifts, and this is when the work is prone to falter. Our study has suggested that faltering at this time might come from a number of causes: structural inflexibility, lack of training, socioeconomic factors, missionary resistance and national church resistance.

Structural inflexibility

In some cases, the denominational structures are such that ongoing authority is retained by an overseas' governing body rather than by national workers. This sort of ethnocentric policy has been the downfall of missions since before the time of Henry Venn. It leads to dependency or to rebellion; national workers either submit to missionary leadership, avoiding responsibility, or they revolt against international domination, leading to desertion or church secession. Even if the national church leaders do not rebel against international domination, the mission field is subjected to remote, and therefore, sub-standard leadership. Overseas administrators cannot expect to lead a national church better than trained nationals since they cannot fully understand the culture or the complexity of local issues and they cannot respond to crises as promptly as those on the scene.

Lack of training

Failure to progress from Stage 3 to Stage 4 may come about because the national worker has not been prepared for leadership. There is a difference between being trained at bible school to go and pastor a village church and being educated to a world standard to navigate national or international issues of funding and leadership. The preparation needed is primarily academic, but it is enhanced by other factors such as linguistic training and exposure to international settings and relationships. If it is important for a missionary to learn the local language on the field, then it is equally important for national leaders to be competent in the language of the church's international business meetings. If a missionary is expected to have a Master's degree to teach at a bible college, then an African also needs a Master's degree to fill the same position. Simply stated, if the national worker is to replace the missionary who is being redeployed, the national worker needs equivalent qualifications.

Socioeconomic factors

Sometimes the lack of prepared leaders is not because none have been trained. In some situations, they were trained, but after training, they did not return to serve the church. When a country, as a whole, lacks educated leaders, this will always be a tension. The best workers can go to government employment, to ministry with denominations that pay better salaries, or they can simply remain overseas after completion of their studies. This requires grace and perseverance, but it can also be greatly relieved by economic empowerment so that appropriate salaries are available for trained workers.

Missionary resistance

Some missionaries have the gift of delegation, and some don't. It takes a special gift to step back and allow others to lead, especially when you have been the leader for some years. If the missionary is not willing to release real authority, the work will rarely progress beyond Stage 3. One symptom of this blockage is when the missionary is committed to having things done "right", which usually means that things are done in a way that meets the missionary's approval. The presence of long-term missionaries, so essential to the early ministry of reaching a foreign culture, potentially becomes the greatest hindrance to progression beyond Stage 3. Progression beyond this point depends upon the missionary's ability to embrace the higher priority of empowering the national church.

Delegation is difficult. The decisions of the new national leadership will not always be acceptable to the mission council. However, that should be when the missionaries can draw upon the satisfaction of achieving their higher priority: seeing the national workers make difficult decisions as strong leaders.

Departure is difficult. Leaving home for the mission field involves an element of self-sacrifice, but in most cases, it is substantially more difficult to conclude your missionary service and return home when your task is complete. Retiring missionaries leave ministries of influence and significance, they leave friends that they have known for much of their adult life, and they leave countries that they have grown to call home. They return to a culture for which they are no longer equipped and where they are not guaranteed any significant role.

National church resistance

The national church may not want to accept the responsibility that comes with increased authority. They may continue to acquiesce to the missionaries, even when national church workers are given the titles of leadership. Equally, national church workers have likely been converted and discipled under the missionary and their own culture may make it very difficult to assume authority from the missionary. In this case, a real transition of power is unlikely to occur while long-term missionaries remain in full-time residence on the field.

Progress falters at Stage 4

A clear application of *The 5 Stages of Missions* model is that the role of missionaries must change as the national church progresses, and the greatest change comes between Stages 3 and 4. At this time it is not simply the tasks of the missionaries that change, but it is their very ownership of the field. Changing leadership titles alone will not effect the required change. For real leadership change to occur, both national workers and missionaries must embrace the new paradigm. National church leaders and missionaries can both be guilty of undermining the leadership change, and sometimes the missionaries will have to leave before change is truly possible.

At least in past centuries, it was almost essential for early missionaries to stay for some decades on the field to be effective. The enormous tasks of language and culture learning support this proposal, as does the use of mission stations as the primary mission strategy. However, as the national church grows, longevity of missionary service can become a handicap. Furthermore, the field missionary may not be the best person to render an objective assessment of the level of maturity of the national church.

Let us illustrate this proposal with a hypothetical mission field from the colonial era. The first missionaries arrived on the field where they have few friends and where they did not know the language or culture. These missionaries spent their first term of service on the field, perhaps four years, learning the language and building contact within the culture so that they could find a place to locate the mission station. They spent the next eight years with two primary activities: construction of mission station buildings and village evangelism. During this time, they recruit specialist medical and educational missionaries to provide immediate care and development in their community. After their first decade they begin to really make progress. The community leaders have accepted them because of the way they are developing health and education. A few of their early converts have shown exceptional commitment and are now in pastoral service. The ministry is beginning to multiply. The missionary provides stability and credibility for the work. His or her growing influence opens doors in the local community and to the international church. The work progresses with increasing momentum, until Stage 4 is reached. Now it is time for the missionary to fade into the background so that the emerging national leaders can assume leadership. The difficulties are small at first. Community leaders show an unwillingness to accept a new proposal until the missionary endorses the idea. The missionary expresses some reservations about a new national church proposal because of international funding constraints. The national church leadership has to change the national board agenda because they still depend upon the (subordinate) missionaries for transport to meetings. Eventually a tear in relations is caused when emerging national leaders challenge the senior missionaries, or simply go and work elsewhere. The missionaries are offended that national church leaders cannot accept advice. And so, the work plateaus or declines.

John the Baptist understood the principle of shifting roles when he said, "he (Jesus) must become greater; I must become less" (John 3: 30). If mission agencies ignore this principle, but rather adopt the policy that "they must increase; we shall remain the same", then they have sown the seeds of failure. The difficulty is that longevity of missionary service has long been portrayed as the sign of a good missionary, when in fact; the best missionary might be the one who sacrifices his or her own career and retires from the field. Consider the assumptions made in the following statement: "My wife and I recently met a missionary who had served in France for over fifty years. We were impressed by his longevity and wanted to know the secret of his successful missionary service" (Smith, 2002: 480). Why was the assumption that fifty years constituted a successful missionary career? Would he have been considered successful if he had achieved the same result in just ten years, and had then gone home to pastor a church?

It is possible for a missionary to remain on the field during the transitions through Stages 3 to 5, but it will require a concerted effort to demonstrate submission to the new leadership. If the missionary is willing, they can take the lead in modelling deference to the new national leader. Furthermore, the easy assumption that "longevity equals success" necessitates the re-education of the missionary, the mission agency and the home church if we are to facilitate national church maturity.

The issue of longevity must be presented carefully. Each type of missionary is essential in his or her own time. Those who pioneered mission fields paid an enormous personal price for their faithfulness. They are truly heroes and heroines of the Faith. However, those who came later, and for the goal of indigenization have accepted relocation, are equally heroic. It is neither wise nor reasonable to judge one generation by the conditions on the field in another generation.

We have not explored the question of whether mission stations are still a legitimate tool of missionary work. Perhaps they are a relic of a former colonial era, or perhaps they are more universally effective. The outcome to a discussion on the continued role of mission stations impacts longevity of missionary service though, since a major portion of the early missionary's time was spent in construction and maintenance of the station. Furthermore, modern technology, multi-media, communications and travel all impact the discussion of longevity. Perhaps, in this shrinking global community, there are simply fewer *Unbridged Missions* situations than there used to be. Perhaps what genuinely took fifty years in past centuries could be achieved in ten years today. The reality is that mission work is changing, whether it is through the maturing of the mission field or through global technological development, and the role of missionaries must be regularly reviewed to meet the need of the time.

Eras of Missions

It is noteworthy that the past century of mission work has taken place during a time of social and philosophical change. For example, the growing unease with any form of colonialism has greatly impacted missions. The increase in literacy levels since the earliest missionaries arrived and the rising affluence of the Western Church have factored in new dynamics in missions. The relevance of these changes to our study lies in the fact that mission work that was started 100 years ago was launched with a radically different ethos to missions today. Therefore, the completion of the mission task is not simply a case of working through a process of five stages. It most likely includes a whole change of mind-set, from colonial philanthropy to international partnership. Anderson and Venn make it clear that exit was always an expectation for early missionaries, but perhaps international partnership was unimaginable.

To illustrate the enormity of the change that mission practice has undergone in the past century, we can consider the changing eras of missions as seen in the development of the Pilgrim Holiness Church[2].

---

[2] The Pilgrim Holiness Church merged with the Wesleyan Methodist Church to form the Wesleyan Church, with whom the author has served. In its early years of existence, the Pilgrim Holiness Church was influential in North American mission development, in a measure disproportionate to its size. The evolution of the Pilgrim Holiness mission culture provides a fascinating sample of North American mission strategy.

Faith Missions

The Pilgrim Holiness Church was founded as a union of small groups committed to holiness. They considered themselves to be a camping movement, drawing support from a wide range of denominations at holiness camp meetings. The resulting small groups had not yet withdrawn from their former denominational membership. In its earliest form, the International Holiness Union and Prayer League "was an interdenominational fellowship. It was not considered to be a denomination or the beginning of one... It might perhaps better be described as a nondenominational society" (Thomas & Thomas, 1976: 14–16). Yet, before it had denominational structures in place, the Union was already sending out missionaries. In fact,

> It is not correct to speak of "sending out" missionaries in the beginning. It would be more accurate to say that the early missionaries "went forth," than to say they were "sent out." They went out under the impulse of their own convictions and to the places where they felt God was calling them. Other individuals felt led to provide the finance. Usually some holiness association like the International Holiness Union and Prayer League certified as to their character and standing but made little attempt to supervise them. The main qualification was to be "saved, sanctified, and called" (Thomas & Thomas, 1976: 29).

This naturally grew out of preaching that, "Any profession of holiness or a spirit-filled life that was not manifested by a burden for reaching the lost both at home and abroad was branded as false" (Thomas & Thomas, 1976: 25).

These independent missionaries went forth as *Faith Missionaries*. The *Faith Missions* era was greatly influenced by Rev. Martin Knapp, who was a cofounder of the Union with Rev. Seth Rees. Knapp lived by faith as a pastor and vigorously promoted the concept in all spheres of Christian work. "Going out by faith was interpreted to mean going out without any definite plans for financial support. Living by faith meant living without any fixed salary or guarantee of support" (Thomas & Thomas, 1976: 34). In Knapp's teaching, Jesus Christ called the missionary; Jesus Christ assigned the missionary; and Jesus Christ promised to support the missionary.

Knapp also founded God's Bible School in Cincinnati, Ohio in 1900. At this missionary training school, it was taught that "gospel workers should not work for any fixed salary but work by faith on a love-offering basis" (Thomas & Thomas, 1976: 34). Two of the earliest students at God's Bible School were Charles and Lettie Cowman, who together with Juji Nakada and Earnest Kilbourne were the founders of the Oriental Missionary Society. Because of the teaching received at God's Bible School, the Cowmans withdrew from their earlier plans of missionary service with the Methodist Board of Missions, were ordained by Rees and Knapp, and went out to serve as *Faith Missionaries* to the Orient. OMS still regards itself as a *Faith Mission* today.

In this era a missionary might well expect to die on the mission field. These ones were living martyrs who made little or no provision for retirement. Choosing mission work was a supreme act of faith. *Faith Missionaries* trusted Christ to provide their needs and in return, followed Christ to wherever he led.

However, the era of *Faith Missions* was short-lived in the International Holiness Union and Prayer league. The virtue of missionary service without guaranteed financial support was dealt a mortal blow when Knapp died of typhoid fever in 1901. It was not long before the International Holiness Union and Prayer League, now the International Apostolic Holiness Union found reasons to move away from this early heritage. It should be noted though, that while the Pilgrim Holiness denomination was evolving in North America, they already had *Faith Missionaries* stationed on three continents and the concept of the living-martyr missionary was well embedded.

Career Missions

The shift away from *Faith Missions* came about at the same time as a rapid change of leadership in the Union in North America. Knapp died in 1901, and in 1905, Rees resigned from leadership. In fact, at the 1905 conference there was a complete change of senior leadership. One reason given was because of the tensions caused by the lack of organizational structure in the Union (Thomas & Thomas, 1976: 51). In 1913 the Union formally structured itself as a denomination and the International Apostolic Holiness Church was formed.

The growing demand for structure had a far-reaching impact. Membership commitments were instituted, and the missionary work was drawn into a stronger organization. Previously in 1897, as a nondenominational union, the group had boasted no membership rules except "the possession of a pure heart" or the sincere desire for the same (Thomas & Thomas, 1976: 16). However, in 1906, membership rules were introduced which included abstinence from the sale or use of tobacco and alcohol, as well as prohibitions against dancing and gambling and attendance at theatres and base-ball games (Thomas & Thomas, 1976: 55).

Furthermore, *Faith Missions* was perceived to be a hindrance to denominational growth. "The deep-seated individualism encouraged by an overemphasis on the individual aspect of the Spirit's leadership was a major obstacle in establishing a permanent organization" (Thomas & Thomas, 1976: 30). In 1905, The Foreign Missionary Board was established to govern missionary work. Missionaries were no longer to be independent but were to fulfill their part in a broader denominational plan of missions. This was especially relevant to the work in South Africa and India, where all of the work started before 1905 is said to have "ended in failure, insofar as the establishing of permanent work was concerned" (Thomas & Thomas, 1976: 68–69). Although it took until 1922 to bring the denomination's missionary giving under central administration, it was clear by that time that missionaries had moved into a new era where missionary service was a career choice. Missionaries were now assigned by the church and supported by the church. Their financial support was guaranteed by the denomination. An example of the denomination's commitment during this era of *Career Missions* is evidenced, when in 1930 the Pilgrim Holiness Church designated a staggering 81% of its North American general church budget to missions (Thomas & Thomas, 1976: 138). *Career Missions* was characterized by loyalty; the missionaries were loyal to the denomination and the denomination was faithful to its missionaries. In this era a missionary might expect to serve on a number of fields during his or her missionary career before returning home to serve at head office or being retired to a denominational retirement village. Choosing mission work was a career choice, rather than martyrdom.

In 1924 and 1925 the International Apostolic Holiness Church merged with two other smaller denominations and adopted the name of the Pilgrim Holiness Church. In 1946 they merged with The Holiness Church, and in 1968 they merged again with the Wesleyan Methodists to form the Wesleyan Church. With merger into the Wesleyan Church came a significant change in missionary funding policy. It was argued that local churches would give directly to appeals for missions, and that the general church budget should no longer serve as a channel for mission giving. From 1968 until 2007, the North American Wesleyan Church contributes 0% of its general budget to overseas' missions. By this action the denomination began to back away from its side of the commitment in *Career Missions*, and although it was to take some decades, mission work moved into yet another era.

Employment Missions

The theory that local churches would contribute directly to a centralized mission budget was probably workable in 1968 since the loyalty factor still motivated general mission giving. However, the profile of the church was changing and general giving to a denominational mission budget gradually decreased. This came to a head in 1990 when a budgetary crisis resulted in several missionary families being brought home from the mission field. This was especially true for the Zambian mission field in Africa, which until that time had maintained a presence of up to 30 missionary families.

The irony was that the decline in general mission giving came about at a time when the denomination was increasing in strength. In this period several of the local churches began to exceed an average attendance of one thousand people. A new dynamic began to appear. Wesleyan churches of two or three thousand adherents began to function almost as separate entities. Their mission giving diversified to missionaries serving with a range of other agencies because of personal connections within the congregation and they began to place more of their giving power behind their own short-term mission teams. This shift occurred in an era when neglect of traditional holiness teaching was resulting in less denominational distinction, and therefore, less loyalty to Wesleyan Missions.

In 1993, as a result of the financial crisis, Global Partners was forced to overhaul their missionary support policy. Each missionary unit was now required to raise a portion of the whole departmental budget in the form of pledges spanning their entire term on the field. When missionaries visited the local churches, they asked for five-year commitments to their particular missionary family. Missionaries were not released to go to the field until their share of the overall departmental budget was in place. A new ethos had evolved where funding was no longer guaranteed by the denomination, and consequently a lifetime career as a missionary could not be guaranteed. The era of *Employment Missions* had arrived. It should be noted that an attitude shift had also taken place in the minds of missionaries as well. Air travel and communication advances reduced the isolation of the missionary. In this era a missionary might expect to serve a section of his or her working years on the mission field, while still retaining employment prospects in the home country.

In more recent years, with the decrease of personnel going to third-world fields in Africa or Latin America and the increase of personnel going to more expensive locations like Russia, Europe and Japan, the budgeting system has again been overhauled. In 2003, Global Partners shifted to a system of personalized budgets, where each missionary family raises an individual budget required for their ministry, rather than a set portion of the overall department's projected budget. Under this new system a missionary can be brought home from the field at any time during the course of the term of service if their actual income drops below their budget (Global Partners, 2005: 3).

The changing ethos of missionary service can be summarized by the following table.

The changing eras of missions

Faith Missions called by Jesus	Living Martyrs: future needs in the hands of Jesus.
Career Missions assigned by the Mission	Loyalty to the agency: future needs cared for by the mission.
Employment Missions employed for a task	Performance based employment: future needs cared for personally.

These changes have been necessary as the Church has attempted to keep up with changing times, and no doubt it is a healthy thing for an organization to keep re-evaluating its procedures and adjusting to meet current financial issues. However, the outcome of reduced "loyalty" giving from Wesleyan churches in a structure where the denomination offers no general support is that the missionaries now raise their own budget while also contributing to the support of staff based at the U.S. headquarters. The concept that career missionaries were supported by the denominational budget has been reversed to the extent that today the denominational mission structures are supported by the missionaries' budgets. The fear today is that missionaries from the North American church have become too expensive to maintain.

Despite the financial difficulties raised by the changing eras of missions, the trend with missionary service is consistent with the need of mission fields. In the early stages, missionaries stayed for decades to learn language and culture, to bring education and to establish the young church. However, in the later stages, the development of national leadership is facilitated more readily by missionary service of limited terms. Continuity and field vision are provided by national leaders, not missionaries.

In the course of discussions with other missionaries, it has been suggested that a fourth era of missions is already becoming evident: that of Tent-Maker Missions. In the 21st century, with the disintegration of denominational loyalty and with the rising cost of sending Western missionaries, more Christians are turning to self-support through employment as a practical way of residing on the mission field.

Tent-Maker Missions would appear to have much in common with early Faith Missions. The missionaries are more readily deployed and are less accountable to denominational structures. However, they would vary from Faith Missionaries in that they don't expect martyrdom and they don't necessarily maintain ties to groups of believers in their home countries. It will be interesting to see whether this suggestion becomes a significant force in future missionary outreach.

Superimposing the *Eras of Missions* onto *The 5 Stages of Missions* demonstrates these trends in missionary work.

Eras of Missions superimposed on 5 Stages (App. E)

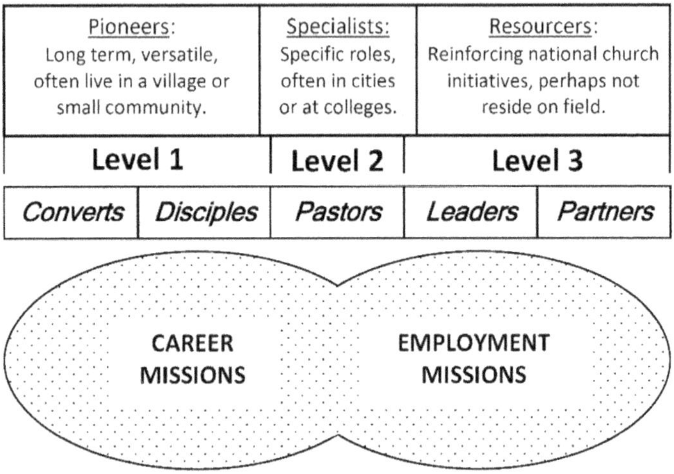

Pioneers: Long term, versatile, often live in a village or small community.		Specialists: Specific roles, often in cities or at colleges.	Resourcers: Reinforcing national church initiatives, perhaps not reside on field.	
Level 1		**Level 2**	**Level 3**	
Converts	*Disciples*	*Pastors*	*Leaders*	*Partners*

CAREER MISSIONS

EMPLOYMENT MISSIONS

Chapter 6: Sharing resources

As the mission field grows to a high level of maturity, a greater degree of self-sufficiency is expected. With this expectation of self-sufficiency often comes a question of dependency: "Does international funding have any place in the developing relationship between the mission and the field?" The answer to this question is not a simple "yes" or "no". The answer lies in a better understanding of *empowerment* and of *partnerships*. While each of these is a substantial topic on its own, a brief overview of the goal of missions will assist in establishing healthy international churches.

The goal of missions

The goal of missions could be described as two-fold: "evangelistic outreach and church planting" (Smith, 1998: 441). First, missions generally commence with a desire to share the Gospel with the lost. However, missions that does not progress beyond evangelization to discipleship and multiplication is unhealthy missions and ultimately, unproductive missions. Hence missions cannot only be about evangelization.

The second goal of missions is therefore, church development: the reproduction of international believers and international churches with their own capacity to do missions beyond themselves. In fact, it might be argued that the second goal is more biblically correct than the first since Jesus never instructed us to go and make converts, but rather to go and make disciples. Likewise, Paul instructed Timothy to disciple "reliable men who will also be qualified to teach others" (2 Timothy 2: 2). Church development is achieved when disciples are mature and reproducing. This truth is captured by Dr. Ebbie Smith, "The goal of missionary activity is the incorporation of responsible, reproducing believers into responsible, reproducing churches" (Smith, 1998: 446). This does not suggest that conversion is unnecessary for discipleship. Rather, the very command to make disciples implies the initial task of making converts. Sadly, the converse is not always practiced; the work of making converts does not always lead to the work of making disciples.

Empowered disciples and empowered churches

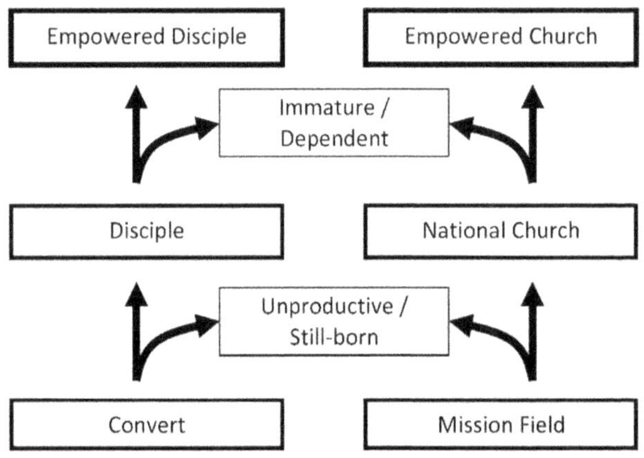

The 5 Stages of Missions highlights the need to include *empowerment* in the completed work of church development. *Empowerment* is the sharing of authority and resources so as to enable growing and lasting strength in the receiving group. Many mission agencies today are discovering that *empowerment* is missions done well, while in contrast, *dependency* is missions done poorly. A disciple who is

indoctrinated, but is not equipped emotionally, intellectually or economically to carry forward the work of missions is an unproductive disciple. Likewise, a mission field that accepts a denominational label but is not empowered is an immature and dependent church. Therefore, our goal is to foster empowered disciples and churches.

The 5 Stages of Missions directs the work of missions to the ultimate goal of establishing a new force in the international church arena – a "self-governing, self-sustaining and self-propagating" body of believers who have become full partners in the task of global evangelization. This work starts with evangelism, requires support for a time, and culminates in a fully equipped international army mobilized for multiplied ministry. The relationship between the mission agency and the mission fields must progress beyond a parental relationship to find fulfillment as a brotherhood of international churches.

The empowered church

Armed with a vision for successful missions, the discussion can then turn to how resources might be best used to achieve that purpose. The use of all available resources to initiate a new mission field is not usually questioned. The questions start when the mission field has achieved some level of maturity. At that point sometimes-painful decisions must be made about the field's ability to fund its own ministries. In fact, at that stage the continuation of non-strategic international funding ceases to help, but rather limits the healthy development of the national church. It can encourage the national church to remain in a child-like state of dependency when it should be taking responsibility for itself.

This unhealthy support is often perpetuated by the mission agency itself, because it can use ongoing funding as a way to retain control for longer than is necessary. This unhealthy, prolonged support is not just demonstrated in the use of money. We also see it in the continued presence of missionary personnel when there are national workers who could be assuming the work. At the 2002 Manzini summit (referred to in chapter 3), the Zambian delegation clearly articulated that they sometimes have to retain missionary personnel because that is the only way to continue to receive international funding. It is usually accepted that money follows missionaries, since missionaries have access to international donor churches. In such a case, the continuation of funding does not produce an empowered church. It has the opposite effect; it produces dependency and a loss of self-image (Smith, 1998: 445).

The question that naturally follows then is, "Are there ways that we can continue to share our resources that will assist the national church beyond dependency and on to full participation in the international arena?" Again, a discussion about money in missions should be no different to a discussion about the deployment of missionary personnel. There is no simple rule for when money or missionaries should be withdrawn from a mission field; there is only the question of how they can best be used to fulfill the goal of an empowered international church.

To better illustrate the progress of a mission field onto full participation in the international work, we can describe two distinct phases: the phase where resources are used to develop the new church and, if missions is done correctly, the phase when resources are used in partnership with the new church to reach out to a third party.

Scaffolding & Partnering in mission relationships

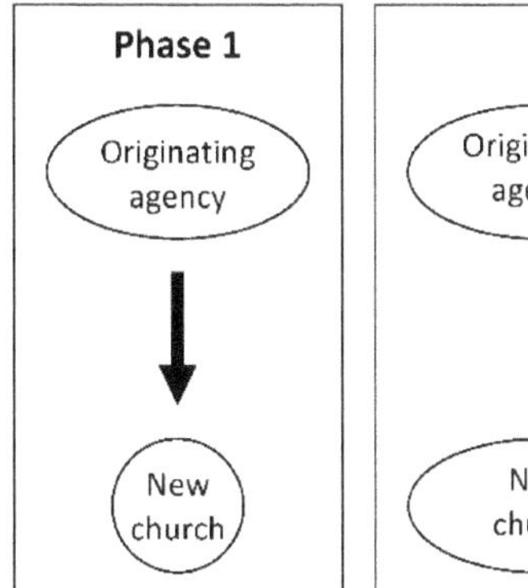

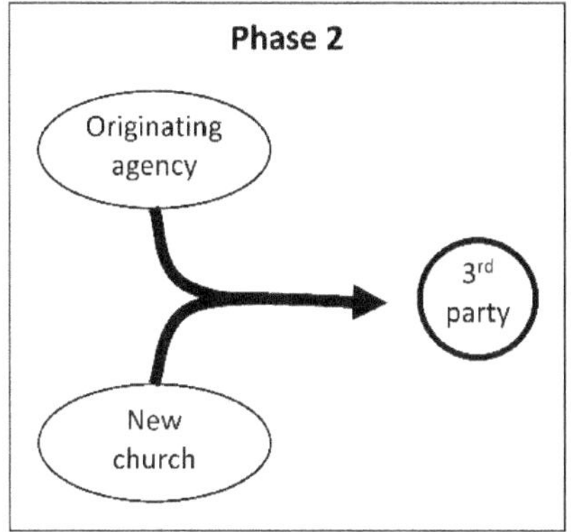

The way that resources (particularly money and missionary personnel) are used in the two phases is different. There are different goals and there are different dynamics at play. In phase 1 there is a paternal relationship between a mature body and an immature body. One body is beholden to the other, as a beneficiary is obligated to a benefactor; a client to a patron. There is a hierarchical relationship since the mission agency carries the authority and the responsibility for development. However, in phase 2, both bodies must learn a new way of relating as peers, based on the knowledge that each needs the other to adequately reach out to the third group. Hierarchical structures are inappropriate in phase 2, because hierarchical structures undermine the goal of shared responsibility. Learning to accept responsibility is part of maturity, and responsibility cannot be passed on to the new church unless real authority is released at the same time.

Partnership is the term most often used to describe the relationship pictured in phase 2. *Partnership* is a very helpful concept, yet its uncritical adoption means that it is often misused. A partnership should include two parties that can relate as peers and work together as each contributes. When a stronger group is simply helping a weaker group, as in phase 1, it should not be designated as a partnership. In that case it is a paternal relationship; a charitable relationship. One is the giver and the other is the receiver. To borrow a term that Henry Venn coined, phase 1 can be labeled as the *scaffolding* phase; when the originating agency is helping build the new church (Henry Venn, as quoted in Shenk, 1977a: 481). The *partnering* phase is reached when the new church achieves a level of maturity where it can contribute in a meaningful way to the work of reaching a third party. Tom Steffen describes partnerships with "agreed upon assigned roles that foster complementary participation" (Steffen, 2000: 727).

A caution in this discussion is that care should be taken not to confuse "mature" with "self-sufficient". The Church should always be insufficient in itself to the task, until the whole world is won. The North American Church is insufficient to the task of world evangelism just as much as the Liberian Church is insufficient to the task. One country may have available personnel, another may have available financial resources, another may have linguistic and cultural ability, and another may have a more consistent habit of prayer. *Partnering* is the bringing together of varied resources for the purpose of achieving what would otherwise be insurmountable for any one group. It is not a contradiction to be mature and still needing assistance. One might argue that true maturity is being able to identify and acknowledge where assistance is still needed. All could use some assistance, at any phase or stage of development. Nonetheless, it is a contradiction to be mature and still want others to do what one is capable of doing oneself.

Interdependence is neither dependency nor individualism (Smith, 2000: 270).

Unless the church and mission leadership have a clear vision of the goal of missions, and unless they also recognize what phase the mission relationship has reached at any given time, the discussion about sharing resources is destined for confusion.

However, in identifying the phases in the shifting relationship between originating and mission churches, it is not to be implied that *scaffolding* and *partnering* are mutually exclusive phases. On the contrary, there is a progression between them and it is quite possible for both to be occurring at the same time. A mission agency might be providing *scaffolding* in the areas of administration and bible college training, while simultaneously *partnering* with the same field in an evangelistic thrust into a new province or in mission outreach into a neighboring country. This is when the relationship enters a stressful period of changing roles, the same as a father and son go through as the son begins to become a man. This transitional period can be managed more effectively if the transition is achieved as quickly as possible.

If this transition goes beyond one generation of leadership, growing rebellion can be expected from the younger, emerging leadership who have been given to hope that they might be self-governing. In discussions with a former Sierra Leonean missionary, I was told of embarrassing incidents when emerging young national leaders criticized the mission for releasing only partial authority. One such leader accused the missionaries in a public meeting, saying, “You give us the goat, but you hold on to the rope.”

When true partnership is achieved, both parties contribute their resources to the goal of reaching a third party. The originating agency contributes from its strength and the new church contributes from its strength. The partnership achieves what neither unit could have achieved alone, and in this way, both are empowered. The cycle is complete when the agency that provided empowerment is empowered in return. For example, an American mission agency provides funding while an African church provides personnel. The result is a new mission field in a location into which American personnel could not easily enter and in which an African church could not financially sustain a presence. The mission agency that set out to empower a mission field is empowered in return. The mission agency that can truly welcome this mature relationship is the agency that will have less tension during the period of transition.

Progressive empowerment

Further explanation of how a *scaffolding* relationship and a *partnering* relationship can coexist is possible using a model of *Progressive Empowerment*.

There are some things that should be established from the very beginning of a new mission work, while there are some things that necessarily come later in the field's development, as the size of the group increases. For example, tithing should be taught as the primary support base for a local church from the very beginning, but a structured program for theological education will likely come later in the history of the church.

Tithing is arguably the fundamental issue of empowerment in missions. In theory, any church with a membership of ten income-earning families should be able to sustain their own pastor at an equivalent standard to the general community. Unfortunately, tithing is not always taught in the early stages of missions. In personal discussions with a former Mozambican superintendent, I heard how he battled to introduce the principle of tithing into local church life. The greatest resistance to the teaching on tithing came from the previous generation of pastors who had seasonal employment in the South African gold mines. The pastors had trained their poorer village congregations not to tithe because the pastors did not personally need the financial support. The superintendent described incidents when the older pastor would stand in the presence of the visiting superintendent, after a message on tithing, and publicly contradict the superintendent's message because he, personally, did not need the congregation's financial support. Furthermore, in discussions with a South African superintendent, I learned that sometimes it was the early missionaries who instructed the African church that they were "too poor to tithe". After 100 years of missionary presence in Africa, dependency still cripples the church, and pastors are still not consistently paid salaries by their congregations. The biblical practice of tithing does not lift a community out of poverty, but it does empower the local church and it ensures that the pastor is no more poverty-stricken than the rest of the village. Every church can, and should, be taught to tithe from the beginning.

Formalized theological education, however, follows sometime after the planting of the first churches. Those with pastoral gifts are selected from among the disciples and provided with specialist training. Some complete undergraduate studies and a few go on to postgraduate studies. The length of time before a bible college program is established varies according to several factors, including literacy levels, the priority of education, the method of instruction (extension or residential) and the growth of the church. Irrespective of these factors, a fully developed bible college program cannot realistically be expected at the time of the first disciples.

Another aspect of church development that trails behind initial church planting is the organization and support of national administration. Levels of administration evolve as the number of local congregations increases. The funding base for national church administration takes time to develop, even if there is a strong tithing base in local churches. It takes a good number of local churches contributing to the national structure before the national administration is sustained. Likewise, and perhaps more so, church institutions such as medical and educational facilities require an extensive base of donors to function.

These considerations lead to the conclusion that there is a progression in the mission field's ability to sustain its own ministries. This progression might include the following elements:

Progressive Empowerment over time

Many of these ministries may be put in place at an early stage with financial subsidy from the originating mission agency. However, the *Progressive Empowerment* model illustrates the fact that the national church's ability to carry the cost of these ministries is increasing over time.

In fact, some of these milestones may not be achievable without social and economic development in the country itself; factors which are outside the control of the church leadership. Consider how difficult it would be to train personnel to post-graduate level in Mozambique in past decades under twentieth century conditions where children speak an African language in the home and must learn to speak Portuguese once they enter school for all studies. At the end of the century, it was reported that there were no Portuguese ex-colonies that employed an African language in education. (Hyltenstam & Stroud, 1993: 15–16).

Furthermore, having learned Portuguese the student battled against an oppressive regime to achieve a secondary school education. The colonial regime had sought to limit the education of Africans to grade 4.

> In fact, the colonial syllabus was just intended to prepare a handful of 'indigenous' people for some low level jobs in the colonial economy, where they were expected to work accurately but without thinking creatively and without questioning the work they were doing. (Kilborn, 1993: 7)

Even in the post-colonial era, any Mozambicans who reached tertiary level education through Portuguese studies, discovered that the universities leaned heavily upon the use of English texts. "As a matter of fact, in some of these libraries, up to 90% of effective texts are in English" (Eduardo & Uprichard, 1995: 18).

The hindrances to empowerment may have been different in other colonized countries, but they were just as real. The oppressive policy of apartheid or the presence of dictators in post-colonial times limited educational opportunities and trained people to be fatalistic. In Southern Africa, in its first century of mission presence, the Wesleyan Church had prepared and retained just one national worker with a Master's degree and two with Bachelor's degrees. These degrees were attained in the United States of America. The presence of poverty, unemployment, disease, war, low education and discrimination still militate against achieving higher levels of empowerment.

In fact, some levels may never be realistically within the reach of the national church in the foreseeable future. For example, while it is conceivable for institutions such as hospitals, schools, and bible colleges to subsist on fees and church subsidies, they are not likely to achieve significant property expansion without injection of additional funding from external sources. This would be true in North America or Europe as much as it would in Africa, except that in wealthier countries donors are more accessible.

Scaffolding, Partnering & Progressive Empowerment (App. F)

Suppose, then, that the new national church has achieved self-sustainability in the lower levels of the model, and is progressing onto higher levels, despite the handicap of social conditions that compete against self-sustainability. Now introduce the concept that this new church has a growing strength and contribution to an international partnership. The modified model illustrates the church at a given time in its development. In this model the originating mission agency is still providing scaffolding for the purpose of national church administration, while simultaneously partnering with the mission church in church planting in a new location.

Sharing resources in the scaffolding phase

During the *scaffolding* phase giving should be guided by the goal of *empowerment*, not by an emotional response to a need. The softest hearts may in fact do the most harm. A visitor on a short-term mission team may see a need, make arrangements with a local worker, and go home to raise money for that need. But even though a short-term need is met, that approach can lead to negative results. Local ownership can be lost, dependency created, and national leadership undermined. It may also lead to careless management of resources since a distress call to the overseas' donor will often provide extra funding for repairs.

It is preferable to send funds through the national leadership. When a national church structure is in place and international fund-raising is directed through that structure, the national leaders are empowered, and the international donor is protected. National leadership should have authority for approval and prioritization of projects and should be held accountable for management of funds. Administration of projects in this manner affirms the national leadership's role in setting the vision and leading the Church, because a local worker must first make the case to his leadership before any appeal can be made to the international church. The procedure also protects the international visitors from exaggerated or manipulative claims for assistance.

Some general guidelines for giving:

- Never undermine the principle of tithing. If pastoral support must be paid by the mission, such as in a church plant, then it should be on a sliding scale so that tithing is factored in and promoted.

- Never fund a project that the national church can support itself. Sometimes this will mean that a project is done in a simpler style to that which might be expected in the donor's country. This is good. This means that the project is more likely to be reproducible.

• Support the local vision rather than imposing an outsider's vision. It is arrogance to assume that a visitor can arrive on a mission field, assess a situation in a matter of days and devise a solution that locals have missed. Furthermore, even if the visitor was correct, a vision without local ownership has failed before it has begun.

• Always submit to national leadership's approval and prioritization when funding projects. If the donor wants to build a church, but the national leadership wants a vehicle, then the donor is obliged to submit to the national leadership. This can be difficult, but acceptance of this priority will turn a request for funding into an opportunity to show respect for the national leadership. The local workers are then instructed to send their requests to the national leadership for consideration, which also makes them acknowledge national leadership. This is *empowerment*. Visitors who do not like to be bound by national structures on the field probably do not enjoy the leadership structures in their own country either. These people quickly become part of the problem of dependency. It would be better that they did not bring their funds to the mission field at all.

• Avoid secret support of individuals and projects. Whenever possible send funds to the mission field through a national church structure.

• Give preference to ministries that are empowering, such as education, community development and capital projects; giving attention to the priority that the projects will be self-sustainable once established.

Sharing resources in the partnering phase

As the national church grows in strength and enters into partnerships with the mission agency and with other international agencies, a change in style of relating must take place. The attitudes of “equality and mutuality” should define the partnerships (Peters, 1972: 238).

For a constructive and lasting partnership, the following attitudes are essential:

- Humility. Those involved in scaffolding new ministries for an extended time can become accustomed to the prestige of being the donor. If the mission agency or international agency cannot now adopt an attitude of humility themselves, the partnership is going to struggle. The very act of entering into a partnership makes the statement that neither party is equipped to effectively engage in the new task alone. Therefore, acknowledge each partner’s strength and expertise and acknowledge your own inability. Share decision making. Don’t withdraw your support if you do not have your way in decision making.

- Honesty. Sometimes the final symptom of distrust is the temptation to hide funding reserves from other partners. While this might provide a sense of security and control, it speaks of deceit to the partners. When one partner is able to produce unexpected additional funding for needs they value, it quickly establishes the perception that there are always hidden reserves, and a request made often enough and urgently enough will be supplied. A mature and honest relationship works to a budget upon which all have agreed.

- Ingenuity. Explore new methods of achieving old tasks. For example, there must be an African method of missions that does not require a four-wheel drive vehicle and photocopy machine.

- Empathy. Do not require personnel from poorer countries, who live on substantially lower salaries and budgets, to serve as missionaries alongside missionaries from wealthier countries. This is especially essential if the "poorer" team members are expected to give leadership.

To ignore the needs of those who are suffering is not an acceptable response to the fear of dependency. To cease to give is to deny one's obligation to God. However, to give carelessly is equally negligent and potentially destructive. Strategic giving and international partnerships are the future of world missions.

Chapter 7: **Conclusions**

The 5 Stages of Missions model has been affirmed in the course of this text, both by the review of published literature and through the comments of national church leaders. The response from missionaries has generally been more polarized. Those who are involved in the theory of missions or who work as mission administrators have responded warmly. Those missionaries who are on the field practicing their calling have been less vocal in their support. In fact, while some were guarded, others seemed to find the concept quite threatening. They accept the basic progression that the model proposes but they do not want to be heard to criticize former missionaries and they are conscious that the model might be used to bring about their own exit.

Supporting models

The 5 Stages of Missions was the primary focus of this work. However, three other minor models were introduced in support.

Bridged and Unbridged Missions

We have defined two different types of missionary venture to international fields. *Bridged Missions* is outreach to another group when cultural, political or linguistic bridges facilitate rapid communication of the Gospel. *Unbridged Missions* is when barriers of politics, culture, language, literacy and economic disparity introduce substantial hindrances to evangelism and church planting. Furthermore, *Bridged Missions* not only facilitates more rapid entry, but it also enables more rapid development of the ministry toward self-sustainability, and consequently, more rapid exit from the mission work.

The conclusion is not that *Bridged Missions* is wrong, or somehow inferior to *Unbridged Missions*. Perhaps *Bridged Missions* is only common sense and good use of the resources that God has provided.

The Eras of missions

It is not only field strategies, such as might be prompted by *The 5 Stages of Missions*, which influence mission policy. The mission culture in the sending countries has changed over the past century as well and this change has produced new expectations for the missionaries, the mission agencies and the missionary-sending churches. To conceptualize the change in mission culture we have described three eras of missions: *Faith Missions*, *Career Missions* and *Employment Missions*.

The historic details used here are quite specific to the Wesleyan Church, but it is likely that similar principles will apply to other mission agencies. For example, the historic origins of OMS International are touched upon. OMS International still describes itself as “an evangelical, interdenominational faith mission” today (OMS International, 2005). It would be interesting to investigate how closely OMS International still adheres to Charles and Lettie Cowman’s original concept of *Faith Missions*, or to God’s Bible School’s practice. Does OMS send forth missionaries today without organizational supervision, without salary and without a retirement plan? Perhaps OMS has undergone policy revision similar to Global Partners. If that is true for these and other mission agencies, then the *Eras of Missions* model could be a useful tool for attaining new focus.

The 5 Stages of Missions model calls upon missionaries to change roles and places of ministry. The *Eras of Missions* model can help the mission agency and the missionary-sending church to move into the new paradigm as well.

The scaffolding and partnering phases

The relationship between the mission agency and the national church continues to evolve, in much the same way that a parent/child relationship develops from one of outright dependency to mutual support. The identification of the two phases in this process of *scaffolding* and *partnering* assists the mission agency and the national church to formulate appropriate policies.

The *Progressive Empowerment* model was presented to demonstrate how *scaffolding* and *partnering* can be in effect at the same time. A mission agency can be *scaffolding* a national church in some ministries, while also *partnering* with the national church in other ministries.

The implications of this discussion upon *The 5 Stages of Missions* are numerous. The phases of *scaffolding* and *partnering* impact upon the issue of empowerment and the sharing of resources, and the *Progressive Empowerment* model explains why a field may appear to be at several different stages of development at any given time.

The mission that awaits us

While this study may have exposed some particular weaknesses in past methodology, it also offers the encouragement that in many cases the work is close to completion. Progression through the early stages has been systematically achieved; it is in the last two stages that indigenization has stalled. Once the vision of internationalization is clearly in mind the sending church and the national church should be able to conclude the mission work and move forward together into international partnership. Two factors deserve special note, the issues of economic empowerment and internationalization.

Economic empowerment

The issue of economic empowerment was highlighted as a crucial issue for nationalization of the church. The mission must address this concern or be negligent. Economic empowerment can be divided into two issues: the funding base for the church, and the funding base for church institutions.

The funding base for the church must be the tithe in the local congregation, not the international donor. Tithing must be promoted and required from the first worship service. If the mission allows the mind-set that the local people are too poor to tithe in the beginning, then it will be extremely difficult to reverse this perception at a later time. The expectation that funding comes down to us from the top cannot exist beside an expectation that the funding rises up from the grass roots.

The funding base for national church institutions, such as hospitals and schools, presents an even greater difficulty. In an affluent society, or in a well-established denomination, these institutions might be supported through a share of the national church budget, but this is not the situation for most mission fields. Tuition fees do not sustain bible colleges and treatment charges do not sustain hospitals. Even in wealthier countries where service charges might support the real service costs, it cannot be expected to provide for development of infrastructure and personnel. The solution has been a perpetual appeal to international donors for funding. This system of international giving, though greatly needed and appreciated, does not alleviate dependency and it rarely provides sufficient support for planned and sustained growth. This is an area that requires more research. Can institutions develop consistent sources of local funding in a third-world setting? If not, then what alternatives are available to the unaffordable institutional model of ministry that Western mission agencies have introduced?

Mission agencies must include economic empowerment on their agenda for mission work.

Work teams and tent-makers

We have talked briefly about the presence of work teams on the mission field and we have speculated that the next era of missionary deployment might come through a wave of self-employed (tent-maker) missionaries. Both of these are honorable responses to the Christian desire to engage in missions, but both increase the presence of untrained personnel on the mission field. There is a risk that this growing number of lay-persons making relatively brief visits to the mission field could erode any cohesive field strategy and significantly hinder the work of indigenization.

If it can be argued that the former generations of qualified and well-meaning career missionaries have, at times, lost sight of the goal of indigenization in the course of their life's work, how much greater is the risk of confusion when waves of untrained personnel visit a mission field, many for a mere three or four weeks. Extra effort must therefore be expended in training work teams and tent-makers in missiological principles.

Unfortunately, we sometimes see the opposite reality, especially with short term teams. Some members of the team arrive on the field focused upon fulfilling their own goals without giving much thought to the field's goals at all. An increasing number of churches use their mission budget to mobilize teams from within their own congregations so that the church members gain new passion in their Christian faith and new compassion for the suffering in the world, resulting in increased vibrancy in the home church. All of this can be achieved without any reference to whether the teams have contributed to the mission field goals in a constructive way.

Long-term damage to mission field goals can be hidden under a thin mask of developmental projects. If a church building is constructed or a well is dug, the work team members feel that they have done a good job. Meanwhile though, the very same project may have undermined the elected church leadership and eroded national church ownership of the work.

Short-term workers require more training, not less training than career missionaries, because they do not have the luxury of time on the field to learn by experience. However, even familiarity with a model such as *The 5 Stages of Missions* does not guarantee that team members grasp the real issues. The crucial issue in indigenization is that national ownership and national leadership produce a greater lasting benefit than a charitable project.

The best protection for a work team is that they serve under the close supervision and leadership of a career missionary or a strong national worker. Team leaders should promote respect for their hosts, and strongly guard against any attitude of contempt that team members might adopt. Team members often do not understand why missionaries function the way that they do and they especially find it hard to understand why missionaries do not respond to every tragic situation or to every beggar they encounter. Sometimes team members conclude that the missionaries are lazy or uncaring, or that national workers are unqualified, and they bypass the safety of experience. Team members who ignore field leadership can do lasting damage on the mission field.

Those who go as tent-maker missionaries are likely to have a different experience to short-term workers because of the duration of their stay. However, sometimes because of the countries they can access through employment, they will find themselves in places where there are no experienced missionaries and no national church workers. If these tent-makers have also disengaged from church structures in their home country, they are in danger of functioning without any strategic supervision and they may repeat centuries of missiological mistakes.

Churches that are mobilizing work teams and tent-maker missionaries must take seriously the complexity of cross-cultural ministry and the priority of reinforcing strong national church leadership. Those who go with humility and a teachable spirit can be a great blessing, but it will not happen through good intentions alone.

Internationalization

Throughout the study there has been a growing awareness and conviction that the goal of missions is to produce an internationally active body of believers, rather than the removal of missionaries from the field. The ultimate goal of missions is the establishment of another international church, fully engaged in international church leadership and international missions.

The continuing presence of a small number of missionaries in the country, or the total absence of missionaries, is not an accurate criterion for completion of the mission task. Mature self-sustaining national churches may choose to draw upon international personnel in education or other specialist roles. Likewise, the ongoing sharing of resources between countries, including finances, personnel and prayer, should not be considered final criteria. The real test of maturity lies in the depth of national leadership and in a national, mission-driven vision.

The outcome of missions, then, is to develop international partners in the task of global evangelism. In this way the final stage tests the mission agency's church of origin: Is the home church mature enough to accept a grown-up mission field as an equal? Those who sent out the original missionaries must now be willing to accept their international brothers and sisters as peers and leaders.

In as much as the field missionaries are likely to resist the implementation of national leadership at Stage 4, so it is true that former international leaders are likely to resist the progression of national workers to the international arena at Stage 5. Missionaries resist Stage 4 because they lose power at that time. International leaders resist Stage 5 because they are similarly unwilling to relinquish their place of honor to overseas' workers.

However, when international leaders truly embrace the concept of an international church, they are richer for the experience. Here is the ultimate goal and the one of the greatest opportunities of missions: having our own Christianity expanded by leaders from other cultures. Like bread upon the waters, missionary service comes back to bless those who sent out missionaries.

Appendix A: The 5 Stages of Missions

The 5 Stages of Missions describe the major transitions of mission work, from the first converts to a mature international church.

Stage 1 encompasses the preparation and arrival of the missionaries until a nucleus of converts has turned to Christ. In this stage the missionaries focus on the work of evangelism. They are learning language, building relationships and sharing Christ. This stage has traditionally included construction of a mission compound, medical facilities and schools.

The transition to *Stage 2* occurs when converts respond and discipleship, establishing churches and leading local worship services now consumes the missionaries' attention. National believers take on more of the engagement with the unchurched.

Stage 3 develops as local congregations increase and the missionary delegates pastoral and discipleship duties to national pastors and takes on the increasing role of pastoral trainer. In this stage the missionary builds a college program and often relocates on-campus. The missionaries still control leadership of the field until this time.

At *Stage 4* the missionaries relinquish leadership to indigenous personnel. This often includes assisting key leaders to attain post-graduate degrees and usually requires some amount of economic empowerment. This is the most difficult transition because missionaries and national staff resist the leadership transition.

Stage 5 follows as the national leaders develop an increasing profile internationally and the national church formalizes its own efforts of missionary outreach. Some missionary presence may continue in the original field, but only in a supportive capacity.

Converts	***Disciples***	***Pastors***	***Leaders***	***Partners***
First contacts:	***Teach believers:***	***Prepare pastors:***	***Replace & redeploy:***	***International ministry:***
• Relationships • Evangelism • Ministries of compassion • Church planting	• Teaching & preaching • Consecration • Small groups • Literature	• TEE • Bible schools • Ordination • Emerging leaders	• Nationals to post-grad level • Re-assign expatriates • Economic empowerment	• Missions to other cultures • Missions to other nations • International leaders

Appendix B: **The 5 Stages and missionary leadership**

As the national church grows and matures, the role of missionaries should change from that of leadership to that of support staff.

Pioneer missionaries are versatile by necessity, often engaged in construction, mechanics, preaching and emergency medical procedures. With the development of national pastors, the missionaries gradually cease serving in rural or suburban ministries and are likely to be reassigned to institutions and cities to fill specialized needs, such as theological educators or medical personnel. Ultimately contact with the field is served by visiting specialists and work-teams.

The difficulty in the model of declining missionary leadership is that it implies that the longer missionaries are present on a field, the less leadership missionaries should exercise. In reality, the opposite usually occurs. Long-term missionaries exert increasing influence over national church decisions, especially when they still have a primary role in securing international funding. A turnover of missionary personnel or the shift to visiting missionary specialists is often necessary for this final stage of indigenization.

This model captures Flora Belle Slater's strategy:

GET IN
GET AHEAD

GET BESIDE
GET BEHIND
GET OUT

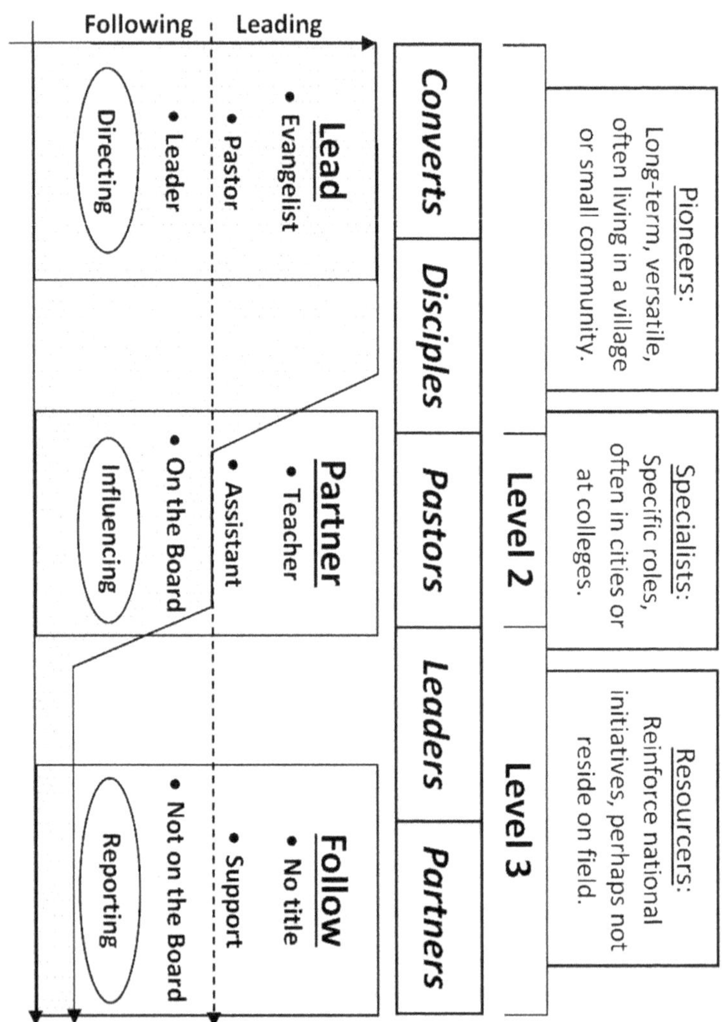

Appendix C: **The 5 Stages diagnostic worksheet**

The 5 Stages of Missions model can be used by missionaries or national church leaders to assess the progress of the national work.

A team or council that is well acquainted with the whole of the national work should complete the diagnostic worksheet and the results consolidated. The results will help to identify

- What stage the work has reached?
- What deficiencies remain in earlier work? and
- What action is required for remedial work or for taking the work onto the next stage?

This is especially helpful during times of transition from missionary to national leadership or when a mission agency is asked to partner with an existing indigenous work.

In the discussion it may become clear that some foundations which were well established in earlier years have been allowed to fall away. It might also be noted, if the work is growing, that different sections of the work are at different stages, requiring different levels of support.

5 Stages of Missions
Diagnostic Worksheet

Date: ___________

Leadership team or Board: ____

3 - Task fully completed and functioning well
2 - Task has been started and only needs minor attention
1 - Task has been started, but needs substantial rework
0 - Very little progress made with task

CONVERTS		**DISCIPLES**		**PASTORS**		**LEADERS**		**PARTNERS**	
First contacts:		***Teach believers:***		***Prepare pastors:***		***Replace & redeploy:***		***International ministry:***	
	3-0		3-0		3-0		3-0		3-0
Relationships		Teaching & preaching		TEE		Nationals to post-grad level		Missions to other cultures	
Evangelism		Consecration		Bible schools		Re-assign expatriates		Missions to other nations	
Ministries of compassion		Small groups		Ordination		Economic empowerment		International leaders	
Church planting		Literature		Emerging leaders					

Appendix D: The goal of missions

If we accept the Great Commission in Matthew 28: 19–20 as the goal of missions, then making disciples might correctly be viewed as the overall goal rather than the second of five stages. Somewhere in the early process of building relationships and modelling the life of faith, the missionary has the joy of seeing the second birth become a reality in one who previously did not know God. The process of discipleship leads the new convert on to growth and to serving others. Some will be called to ministry and to leadership. Some will be called to take the message of Christ to other nations. All will be called to be disciples.

The second implication of the model is that the work of missions cannot truly be the last of five chronological stages. The claim that Christ makes upon our lives is that we share our faith from the earliest knowledge of his gracious provision for our salvation. Converts tell family members about their experience. The pastor takes an active interest in the mission field in the neighboring town or the next tribal group. The leader will spur the church on to outreach and self-sacrifice as a fundamental motivation in the Christian life. Nonetheless, willingness to give up one's own life to preach the Gospel to a foreign people in a foreign land remains one of the ultimate opportunities to follow Christ's example.

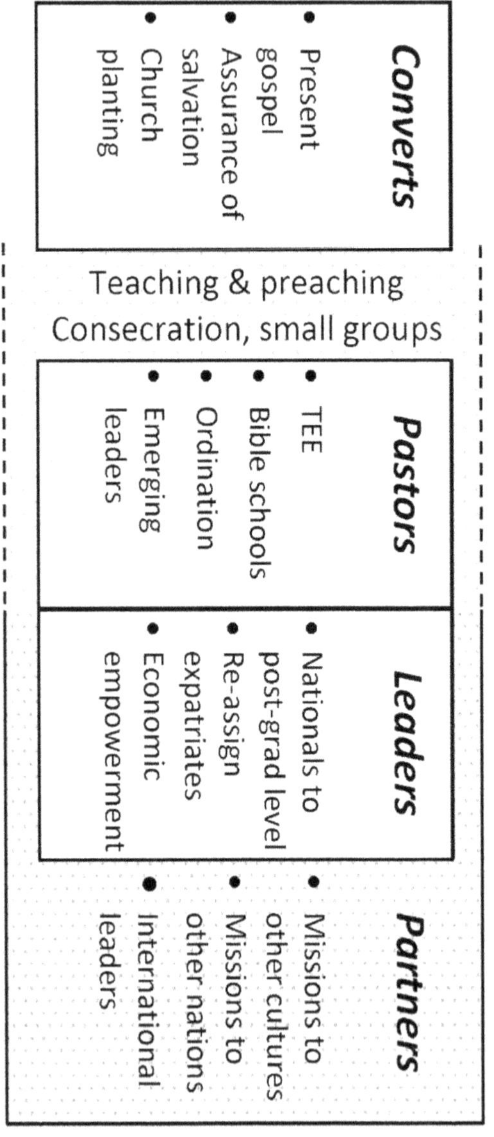
Relationships, Pre-evangelism
Ministries of compassion
Converts
Present gospel
Assurance of salvation
Church planting
Teaching & preaching
Consecration, small groups
Disciples
Pastors
TEE
Bible schools
Ordination
Emerging leaders
Leaders
Nationals to post-grad level
Re-assign expatriates
Economic empowerment
Partners
Missions to other cultures
Missions to other nations
International leaders

Appendix E: **The Eras of Missions superimposed on the 5 Stages**

In two centuries of Protestant missions work, the expectation upon missionaries has changed. Early missionaries paid a high price in their commitment to reach foreign cultures. Many missionaries paid with their lives. Those who returned often came home physically and emotionally broken. The commitment of missionaries was high and so was the commitment of mission agencies. The mutual commitment was for a lifetime. Missionaries who came home were cared for into retirement.

In more recent decades the missionary contract has changed. Missionaries do not necessarily expect to be overseas for their entire career. They maintain communication with their home church and travel home more regularly than ever before. This has resulted in a limited term of commitment between the missionary and the agency. In some cases, it is now considered at-will employment.

This move away from a lifetime commitment to missionary service might be viewed as a great loss, but strangely this change meshes well with the maturing of many mission fields. A missionary who stays on the field until retirement might just be the person who holds up the indigenization of the field for a decade or two. National workers may not step up to leadership roles while a qualified missionary remains. The irony is that the very skills and education that are important for missionaries can become the obstacle to indigenization. To be clear, this might not be because the missionary is unwilling to relinquish responsibilities but because the national workers are unwilling to accept extra responsibilities while a resourced missionary is still so available.

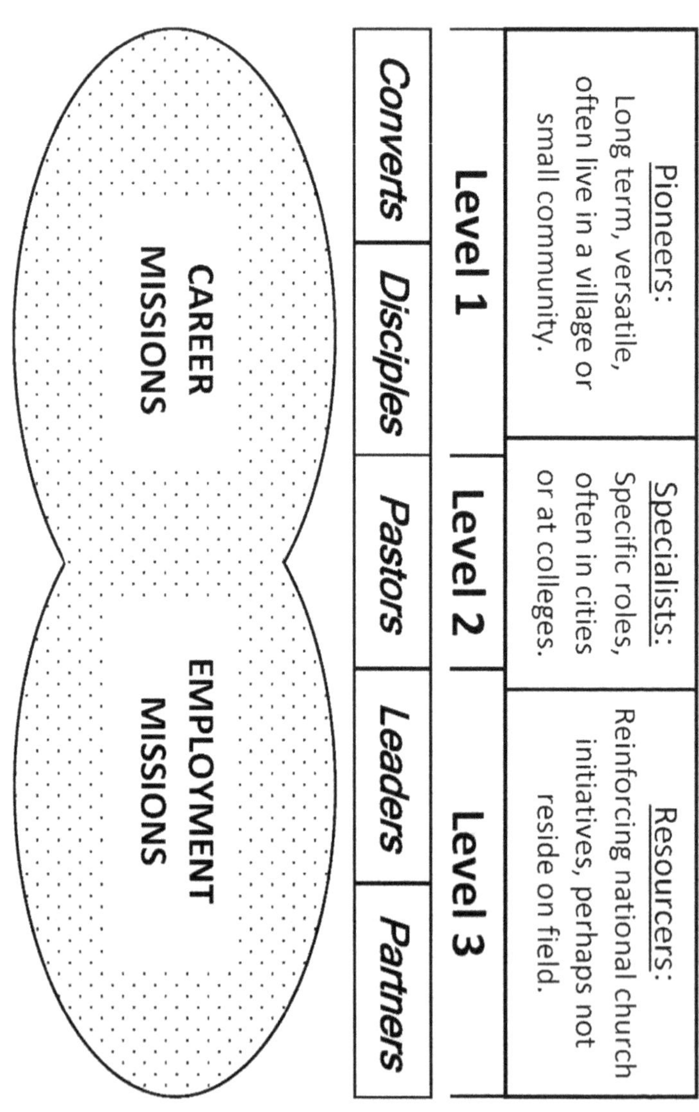

Appendix F: Scaffolding, Partnering & Progressive Empowerment

There are some ministries on the mission field that take much longer to indigenize than others. Institutions especially, such as colleges, hospitals and schools, require more funding than many fields can afford. A national church will not usually become financially independent of its national economy, so a church in a poor country will generate small tithes and low pastoral wages. This will provide for local church ministries but will not quickly provide for the overheads required for institutions. International scaffolding for institutions may be an ongoing necessity, and this must somehow be separated from the concept of indigenization of the ministry.

Meanwhile, the capacity of national workers may quickly surpass the effectiveness of missionaries. National workers should quickly take the lead in ministry in their own villages and may soon take the lead in outreach to other tribal groups and neighboring countries. Some of the suspicion held against Western missionaries may not be held against African, Latin American, Asian or Pacific missionaries. The increasing cost of sending Western missionaries also raises a question over the sustainability of this ministry. In many parts of the world former mission fields are becoming the leaders in missionary outreach. This provides a powerful opportunity for the former mission agency and the national church to partner together with unprecedented effectiveness.

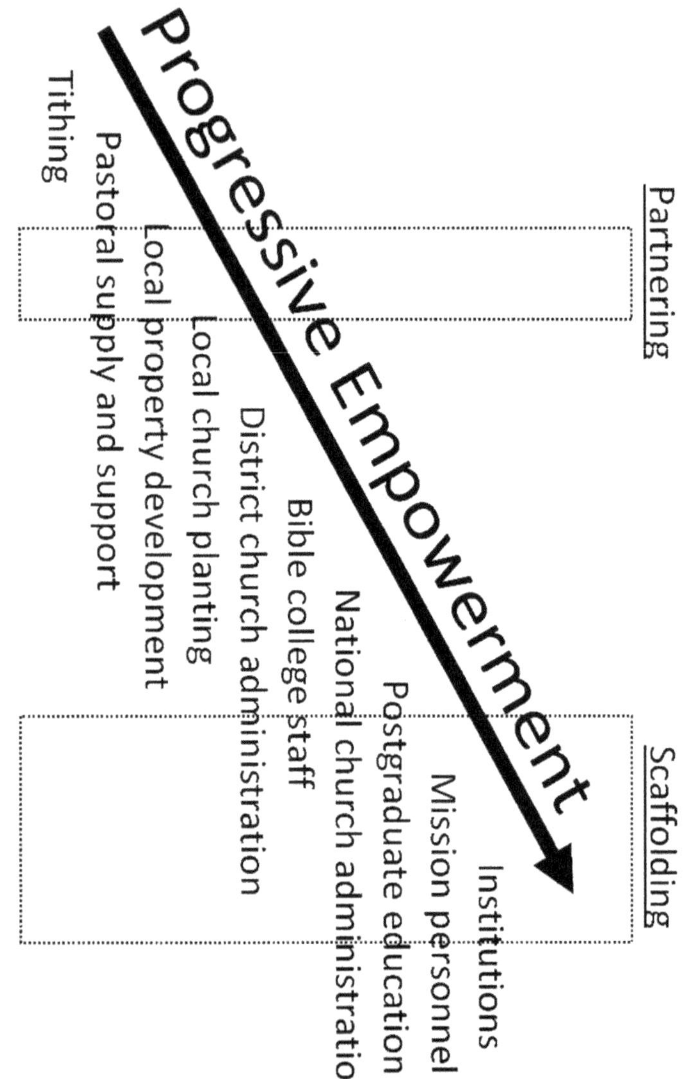
Partnering
Scaffolding
Progressive Empowerment
Institutions
Mission personnel
Postgraduate education
National church administration
Bible college staff
District church administration
Local church planting
Local property development
Pastoral supply and support
Tithing

Reference list

Allen, R 1998. *Missionary Methods: St. Paul's or Ours?* Grand Rapids: Eerdmans.

_______ 1997. *The Spontaneous Expansion of the Church.* Eugene, OR: Wipf & Stock.

Beaver, R 1979. "The Legacy of Rufus Anderson", in *Occasional Bulletin of Missionary Research.* 3(03): 94–97.

Branner, J 1972. "McGavran speaks on Roland Allen" (An interview by John K. Branner), in *Evangelical Missions Quarterly.* 8(3):165–74.

Eduardo, T & Uprichard, E 1995. *The Proceedings of the First National Conference on English Language Teaching in Mozambique*. Mozambique: Ministry of Education.

Finzel, H 1992. "Love 'em and leave 'em: on temporary partnerships and recycling of missionaries", in *International Journal of Frontier Missions* 9(3): 103–05.

Fox, F 2001. "Partnership—more than a buzzword", in *Evangelical Missions Quarterly*. 37(3): 294–304.

Fuller, W 1981. *Mission-Church Dynamics.* Pasadena: William Carey.

Global Partners 2005. *Missionary support system policy & procedure.* http://www2.wesleyan.org/wwm/missionaries2/frms1.php.

Hyltenstam, K & Stroud, C 1993. *Final Report and Recommendations from the Evaluation of Teaching Materials for Lower Primary Education in Mozambique. II. Language Issues*. Mozambique: National Institute for Education.

Kilborn, W 1993. *Final Report and Recommendations from the Evaluation of Teaching Materials for Lower Primary Education in Mozambique. III. Mathematics.* Mozambique: National Institute for Education.

LaTourette, K 1999. *A History of Christianity vol. II. Reformation to the present.* Revised edition. Peabody, MA: Prince.

Mathews, E 1990. "History of missions: a brief survey", in *Journal of Applied Missiology*. 1(1): 297.

McGavran, D 1986. "My pilgrimage in mission", in *International Bulletin of Missionary Research.* 10(2): 53–58.

_______ 1989. "Missiology faces the lion", in *Missiology: An International Review.* 17(3): 335–56.

McLeister, F & Nicholson, S 1976. *Conscience and Commitment: The History of the Wesleyan Methodist Church of America.* Marion, IN: Wesley.

Monsma, T 1994. "What is the bottom line in missions?", in *Mission Frontiers.* http://www.missionfrontiers.org/1994/0910/so9411.htm

OMS International 2005. http://www.omsinternational.org/

Peters, G 1972. *A Biblical Theology of Missions.* Chicago: Moody.

Shenk, W 1977a. "Henry Venn's instructions to missionaries", in *Missiology: An International Review.* 5(4): 467–86.

_______ 1977b. "Henry Venn's legacy", in *Occasional Bulletin of Missionary Research.* 1(02): 16–19.

_______ 1990. "The origins and evolution of the Three-Selfs in relation to China", in *International Bulletin of Missionary Research.* 14(1): 28–35.

_______ 1996. "The role of theory in mission studies", in *Missiology: An International Review*. 24(1): 31–45.

Smith, D 2000. "Dependency", in *Evangelical Dictionary of World Missions*, A Moreau (ed). Grand Rapids, MI: Baker.

Smith, R 2002. "A testimony for missions: respect or rejection", in *Evangelical Missions Quarterly*. 38(4): 480–88.

Smith, E 1998. "Introduction to the strategy and methods of missions", in *Missiology: An Introduction to the Foundations, History, and Strategies of World Missions*, J Terry, E Smith & J Anderson (eds). Nashville: Broadman & Holman.

Steffen, T 1997. *Passing the Baton*. La Habra, CA: Center for Organizational & Ministry Development.

_______ 2000. "Partnership", in *Evangelical Dictionary of World Missions*, A Moreau (ed). Grand Rapids, MI: Baker.

Thomas, P & Thomas, W 1976. *The Days of Our Pilgrimage: The History of the Pilgrim Holiness Church*. Marion, IN: Wesley.

Wagner, C 1971. *Frontiers in Missionary Strategy*. Chicago: Moody.

Wesleyan Church of Sierra Leone 1985. *The Discipline of the Wesleyan Church of Sierra Leone 1985*. Revised Ed. Indianapolis: Wesley.

www.ingramcontent.com/pod-product-compliance
Lightning Source LLC
Chambersburg PA
CBHW071535040426
42452CB00008B/1022